A TREASURY OF
A.W. TOZER

Lord God,
Dear Father and
Saviour of and
Christ our Lord
We come to you
humbly onsday
before your person
in the the
name of JESUS by
the help of respon

A TREASURY OF A.W. TOZER

A Collection of Tozer Favorites

Introduction by
WARREN W. WIERSBE

BAKER BOOK HOUSE
Grand Rapids, Michigan 49506

Printed in the United States of America

Excerpts from *The Divine Conquest*
by A. W. Tozer, Copyright 1950, renewed 1977,
are reprinted by permission of
the Fleming H. Revell Company,
Old Tappan, New Jersey.

Excerpts from *The Knowledge of the Holy*
by A. W. Tozer, copyright 1961 by Aiden Wilson Tozer
are reprinted by permission of Harper & Row,
Publishers, Inc., New York.

All other excerpts from previously published volumes by A. W. Tozer are
reprinted with the permission of Christian Publications, Harrisburg,
Pennsylvania.

Paperback edition, 1981
ISBN: 0-8010-8860-7

Contents

Introduction

"I guess my philosophy is this: Everything is wrong until God sets it right."

That statement from Dr. A. W. Tozer perfectly summarizes what he believed and what he tried to do during his years of ministry. The entire focus of his preaching and writing was on God. He had no time for religious hucksters who were inventing new ways to promote their wares and inflate their statistics. Like Thoreau, whom he read and admired, Tozer marched to a different drummer; and for this reason, he was usually out of step with many of the people in the religious parade.

But it was this evangelical eccentricity that made us love him and appreciate him. He was not afraid to tell us what was wrong. Nor was he hesitant to tell us how God could make it right. If a sermon can be compared to light, then A. W. Tozer released a laser beam from the pulpit, a beam that penetrated your heart, seared your conscience, exposed sin, and left you crying, "What must I do to be saved?" The answer was always the same: surrender to Christ; get to know God personally; grow to become like Him.

Aiden Wilson Tozer was born in Newburg (then known as La Jose), Pennsylvania, on April 21, 1897. In 1912 the family moved from the farm to Akron, Ohio; and in 1915 he was converted to Christ. He immediately entered into a life of devotional intensity and personal witness. In 1919 he began pastoring the Alliance Church in Nutter Fort, West Virginia. He also pastored churches in Morgantown, West Virginia; Toledo, Ohio; Indianapolis, Indiana; and in 1928 came to the Southside Alliance Church in Chicago. Here he ministered until November, 1959, when he became pastor of the Avenue Road Church in Toronto. A sudden heart attack on May 12, 1963, ended that ministry and Tozer was ushered into Glory.

I am sure that Tozer reached more people through his writing than his preaching. Much of his writing was reflected in the preaching of pastors who fed their souls on his words. In May, 1950, he was named editor of *The Alliance Weekly,* now *The Alliance Witness,* which was probably the only religious magazine purchased primarily for its editorials. I once heard Dr. Tozer at an Evangelical Press Association conference taking to task editors who practiced what he called "super-market journalism—two columns of advertising and one aisle of reading material." He was an exacting writer and was as hard on himself as he was on others.

What is there about A. W. Tozer's writings that gets hold of us and will not let us go? Tozer did not enjoy the privilege of a university or seminary training, or even a Bible School education for that matter; yet he has left us a shelf of books that will be mined for their spiritual wealth until the Lord returns.

For one thing, A. W. Tozer wrote with conviction. He was not interested in tickling the ears of the shallow Athenian Christians who were looking for some new thing. Tozer redug the old wells and called us back to the old paths, and he passionately believed and practiced the truths that he taught. He once told a friend of mine, "I have preached myself off of every Bible Conference platform in the country!" The popular crowds do not rush to hear a man whose convictions make them uncomfortable.

Tozer was a mystic—an evangelical mystic—in an age

that is pragmatic and materialistic. He still calls us to see that real world of the spiritual that lies beyond the physical world that so ensnares us. He begs us to please God and forget the crowd. He implores us to worship God that we might become more like Him. How desperately we need that message today!

A. W. Tozer had the gift of taking a spiritual truth and holding it up to the light so that, like a diamond, every facet was seen and admired. He was not lost in homiletical swamps; the wind of the Spirit blew and dead bones came to life. His essays are like fine cameos whose value is not determined by their size. His preaching was characterized by an intensity—spiritual intensity—that penetrated one's heart and helped him to see God. Happy is the Christian who has a Tozer book handy when his soul is parched and he feels God is far away.

This leads to what I think is the greatest contribution A. W. Tozer makes in his writings: he so excites you about truth that you forget Tozer and reach for your Bible. He himself often said that the best book is the one that makes you want to put it down and think for yourself. Rarely do I read Tozer without reaching for my notebook to jot down some truth that later can be developed into a message. Tozer is like a prism that gathers the light and then reveals its beauty.

Warren W. Wiersbe
The Moody Church
Chicago, Illinois

Excerpts from
The Knowledge of the Holy

The Immutability of God
The Justice of God
The Mercy of God
The Sovereignty of God

1

The Immutability of God

O Christ our Lord, Thou hast been our dwelling place in all generations. As conies to their rock, so have we run to Thee for safety; as birds from their wanderings, so have we flown to Thee for peace. Chance and change are busy in our little world of nature and men, but in Thee we find no variableness nor shadow of turning. We rest in Thee without fear or doubt and face our tomorrows without anxiety. Amen.

The immutability of God is among those attributes less difficult to understand, but to grasp it we must discipline ourselves to sort out the usual thoughts with which we think of created things from the rarer ones that arise when we try to lay hold of whatever may be comprehended of God.

To say that God is immutable is to say that He never differs from Himself. The concept of a growing or developing God is not found in the Scriptures. It seems to me impossible to think of God as varying from Himself in any way. Here is why:

For a moral being to change it would be necessary that the change be in one of three directions. He must go from better to worse or from worse to better; or, granted that the moral quality remain stable, he must change within himself, as from immature to mature or from one order of being to another. It should be clear that God can move in none of these directions. His perfections forever rule out any such possibility.

God cannot change for the better. Since He is perfectly holy, He has never been less holy than He is now and can never be holier than He is and has always been. Neither can God change for the worse. Any deterioration within the unspeakably holy nature of God is impossible. Indeed I believe it impossible even to think of such a thing, for the moment we attempt to do so, the object about which we are thinking is no longer God but something else and someone less than He. The one of whom we are thinking may be a great and awesome creature, but because he is a creature he cannot be the self-existent Creator.

As there can be no mutation in the moral character of God, so there can be none within the divine essence. The being of God is unique in the only proper meaning of that word; that is, His being is other than and different from all other beings. We have seen how God differs from His creatures in being self-existent, self-sufficient, and eternal. By virtue of these attributes God is God and not some other being. One who can suffer any slightest degree of change is neither self-existent, self-sufficient, nor eternal, and so is not God.

Only a being composed of parts may change, for change is basically a shift in the relation of the parts of a whole or the admission of some foreign element into the original composition. Since God is self-existent, He is not composed. There are in Him no parts to be altered. And since He is self-sufficient, nothing can enter His being from without.

"Whatever is composed of parts," says Anselm, "is not altogether one, but is in some sort plural, and diverse from itself; and either in fact or in concept is capable of dissolution. But these things are alien to Thee, than whom nothing better can be conceived of. Hence, there are no parts in Thee, Lord, nor art Thou more than one. But Thou art so truly a unitary being, and so identical with Thyself, that in no respect art Thou unlike Thyself; rather Thou art unity itself, indivisible by any conception."

"All that God is He has always been, and all that He has been and is He will ever be." Nothing that God has ever said about Himself will be modified; nothing the inspired prophets and apostles have said about Him will be rescinded. His immutability guarantees this.

The immutability of God appears in its most perfect beauty when viewed against the mutability of men. In God no change is possible; in men change is impossible to escape. Neither the man is fixed nor his world, but he and it are in constant flux. Each man appears for a little while to laugh and weep, to work and play, and then to go to make room for those who shall follow him in the never-ending cycle.

Certain poets have found a morbid pleasure in the law of impermanence and have sung in a minor key the song of perpetual change. Omar the tentmaker was one who sang with pathos and humor of mutation and mortality, the twin diseases that afflict mankind. "Don't slap that clay around so roughly," he exhorts the potter, "that may be your grandfather's dust you make so free with." "When you lift the cup to drink red wine," he reminds the reveler, "you may be kissing the lips of some beauty dead long ago."

This note of sweet sorrow expressed with gentle humor gives a radiant beauty to his quatrains but, however beautiful, the whole long poem is sick, sick unto death. Like the bird charmed by the serpent that would devour it, the poet is fascinated by the enemy that is destroying him and all men and every generation of men.

The sacred writers, too, face up to man's mutability, but they are healthy men and there is a wholesome strength in their words. They have found the cure for the great sickness. God, they say, changes not. The law of mutation belongs to a fallen world, but God is immutable, and in Him men of faith find at last eternal permanence. In the meanwhile change works for the children of the kingdom, not against them. The changes that occur in them are wrought by the hand of the in-living Spirit. "But we all," says the apostle, "with open face beholding as in a glass the glory of the Lord, are changed into the same image from glory to glory, even as by the Spirit of the Lord."

In a world of change and decay not even the man of faith can be completely happy. Instinctively he seeks the unchanging and is bereaved at the passing of dear familiar things.

> O Lord! my heart is sick,
>   Sick of this everlasting change;
>   And life runs tediously quick
>   Through its unresting race and varied range:
>   Change finds no likeness to itself in Thee,
>   And wakes no echo in Thy mute Eternity.
>   Frederick W. Faber

These words of Faber find sympathetic response in every heart; yet much as we may deplore the lack of stability in all earthly things, in a fallen world such as this the very *ability* to change is a golden treasure, a gift from God of such fabulous worth as to call for constant thanksgiving. For human beings the whole possibility of redemption lies in their ability to change. To move across from one sort of person to another is the essence of repentance: the liar becomes truthful, the thief honest, the lewd pure, the proud humble. The whole moral texture of the life is altered. The thoughts, the desires, the affections are transformed, and the man is no longer what he had been before. So radical is this change that the apostle calls the man that used to be "the old man" and the man that now is "the new man, which is renewed in knowledge after the image of him that created him."

Yet the change is deeper and more basic than any external acts can reveal, for it includes also the reception of life of another and higher quality. The old man, even at his best, possesses only the life of Adam: the new man has the life of God. And this is more than a mere manner of speaking; it is quite literally true. When God infuses eternal life into the spirit of a man, the man becomes a member of a new and higher order of being.

In the working out of His redemptive processes the unchanging God makes full use of change and through a succession of changes arrives at permanence at last. In the Book of Hebrews this is shown most clearly. "He taketh away the first, that he may establish the second," is a kind of summation of the teaching of that remarkable book. The old covenant, as something provisional, was abolished, and the new and everlasting covenant took its place. The blood of goats and bulls lost its significance when the blood of the Paschal Lamb was shed. The law, the altar, the priesthood—all were temporary and subject to change; now the eternal law of God is engraven forever on the living, sensitive stuff of which the human soul is composed. The ancient sanctuary is no more, but the new sanctuary is eternal in the heavens and there the Son of God has His eternal priesthood.

Here we see that God uses change as a lowly servant to bless His redeemed household, but He Himself is outside of the law of mutation and is unaffected by any changes that occur in the universe.

> *And all things as they change proclaim*
> *The Lord eternally the same.*
>
> Charles Wesley

Again the question of use arises. "Of what use to me is the knowledge that God is immutable?" someone asks. "Is not the whole thing mere metaphysical speculation? Something that might bring a certain satisfaction to persons of a particular type of mind but can have no real significance for practical men?"

If by "practical men" we mean unbelievers engrossed

in secular affairs and indifferent to the claims of Christ, the welfare of their own souls, or the interests of the world to come, then for them such a book as this can have no meaning at all; nor, unfortunately, can any other book that takes religion seriously. But while such men may be in the majority, they do not by any means compose the whole of the population. There are still the seven thousand who have not bowed their knees to Baal. These believe they were created to worship God and to enjoy His presence forever, and they are eager to learn all they can about the God with whom they expect to spend eternity.

In this world where men forget us, change their attitude toward us as their private interests dictate, and revise their opinion of us for the slightest cause, is it not a source of wondrous strength to know that the God with whom we have to do changes not? That His attitude toward us now is the same as it was in eternity past and will be in eternity to come?

What peace it brings to the Christian's heart to realize that our Heavenly Father never differs from Himself. In coming to Him at any time we need not wonder whether we shall find Him in a receptive mood. He is always receptive to misery and need, as well as to love and faith. He does not keep office hours nor set aside periods when He will see no one. Neither does He change His mind about anything. Today, this moment, He feels toward His creatures, toward babies, toward the sick, the fallen, the sinful, exactly as He did when He sent His only-begotten Son into the world to die for mankind.

God never changes moods or cools off in His affections or loses enthusiasm. His attitude toward sin is now the same as it was when He drove out the sinful man from the eastward garden, and His attitude toward the sinner the same as when He stretched forth His hands and cried, "Come unto me, all ye that labour and are heavy laden, and I will give you rest."

God will not compromise and He need not be coaxed.

He cannot be persuaded to alter His Word nor talked into answering selfish prayer. In all our efforts to find God, to please Him, to commune with Him, we should remember that all change must be on our part. "I am the Lord, I change not." We have but to meet His clearly stated terms, bring our lives into accord with His revealed will, and His infinite power will become instantly operative toward us in the manner set forth through the gospel in the Scriptures of truth.

> *Fountain of being! Source of Good!*
> *Immutable Thou dost remain!*
> *Nor can the shadow of a change*
> *Obscure the glories of Thy reign.*
>
> *Earth may with all her powers dissolve,*
> *If such the great Creator will;*
> *But Thou for ever art the same,*
> *I AM is Thy memorial still.*
>
> *From* Walker's Collection

2

The Justice of God

*Our Father, we love Thee for Thy justice. We acknowledge that
Thy judgments are true and righteous altogether. Thy justice
upholds the order of the universe and guarantees the safety of all
who put their trust in Thee. We live because Thou art just—and
merciful. Holy, holy, holy, Lord God Almighty, righteous in all
Thy ways and holy in all Thy works. Amen.*

In the inspired Scriptures justice and righteousness are
scarcely to be distinguished from each other. The same
word in the original becomes in English *justice* or *righteousness*, almost, one would suspect, at the whim of the
translator.

The Old Testament asserts God's justice in language
clear and full, and as beautiful as may be found anywhere
in the literature of mankind. When the destruction of
Sodom was announced, Abraham interceded for the righteous within the city, reminding God that he knew He
would act like Himself in the human emergency. "That be
far from thee to do after this manner, to slay the righteous
with the wicked: and that the righteous should be as the
wicked, that be far from thee: Shall not the Judge of all the
earth do right?"

The concept of God held by the psalmists and prophets
of Israel was that of an all-powerful ruler, high and lifted
up, reigning in equity. "Clouds and darkness are round

about him: righteousness and judgment are the habitation of his throne." Of the long-awaited Messiah it was prophesied that when He came He should judge the people with righteousness and the poor with judgment. Holy men of tender compassion, outraged by the inequity of the world's rulers, prayed, "O Lord God, to whom vengeance belongeth; O God, to whom vengeance belongeth, shew thyself. Lift up thyself, thou judge of the earth: render a reward to the proud. Lord, how long shall the wicked, how long shall the wicked triumph?" And this is to be understood not as a plea for personal vengeance but as a longing to see moral equity prevail in human society.

Such men as David and Daniel acknowledged their own unrighteousness in contrast to the righteousness of God, and as a result their penitential prayers gained great power and effectiveness. "O Lord, righteousness belongeth unto thee, but unto us confusion of faces." And when the long-withheld judgment of God begins to fall upon the world, John sees the victorious saints standing upon a sea of glass mingled with fire. In their hands they hold the harps of God; the song they sing is the song of Moses and the Lamb, and the theme of their song is the divine justice. "Great and marvellous are thy works, Lord God Almighty; just and true are thy ways, thou King of saints. Who shall not fear thee, O Lord, and glorify thy name? for thou alone art holy: for all nations shall come and worship before thee; for thy judgments are made manifest."

Justice embodies the idea of moral equity, and iniquity is the exact opposite; it is *in*-equity, the absence of equality from human thoughts and acts. Judgment is the application of equity to moral situations and may be favorable or unfavorable according to whether the one under examination has been equitable or inequitable in heart and conduct.

It is sometimes said, "Justice requires God to do this," referring to some act we know He will perform. This is an error of thinking as well as of speaking, for it postulates a principle of justice outside of God which compels Him to act in a certain way. Of course there is no such principle. If there were it would be superior to God, for only a superior power can compel obedience. The truth is that there is not and can never be anything outside of the nature of God which can move Him in the least degree. All God's reasons come from within His uncreated being. Nothing has entered the being of God from eternity, nothing has been removed, and nothing has been changed.

Justice, when used of God, is a name we give to the way God is, nothing more; and when God acts justly He is not doing so to conform to an independent criterion, but simply acting like Himself in a given situation. As gold is an element in itself and can never change nor compromise but is gold wherever it is found, so God is God, always, only, fully God, and can never be other than He is. Everything in the universe is good to the degree it conforms to the nature of God and evil as it fails to do so. God is His own self-existent principle of moral equity, and when He sentences evil men or rewards the righteous, He simply acts like Himself from within, uninfluenced by anything that is not Himself.

All this seems, but only seems, to destroy the hope of justification for the returning sinner. The Christian philosopher and saint, Anselm, Archbishop of Canterbury, sought a solution to the apparent contradiction between the justice and the mercy of God. "How dost Thou spare the wicked," he inquired of God, "if Thou art all just and supremely just?" Then he looked straight at God for the answer, for he knew that it lies in *what God is*. Anselm's findings may be paraphrased this way: God's being is unitary; it is not composed of a number of parts working harmoniously, but simply one. There is nothing in His justice which forbids the exercise of His mercy. To think of God as we sometimes think of a court where a kindly judge, compelled by law, sentences a man to death with tears and apologies, is to think in a manner wholly unworthy of the true God. God is never at cross-purposes with Himself. No attribute of God is in conflict with another.

God's compassion flows out of His goodness, and goodness without justice is not goodness. God spares us because He is good, but He could not be good if He were not just. When God punishes the wicked, Anselm concludes, it is just because it is consistent with their deserts; and when He spares the wicked it is just because it is compatible with His goodness; so God does what becomes Him as the supremely good God. This is reason seeking to understand, not that it may believe but because it already believes.

A simpler and more familiar solution for the problem of how God can be just and still justify the unjust is found in the Christian doctrine of redemption. It is that, through the work of Christ in atonement, justice is not violated but satisfied when God spares a sinner. Redemptive theology teaches that mercy does not become effective toward a man until justice has done its work. The just penalty for sin was exacted when Christ our Substitute died for us on the cross. However unpleasant this may sound to the ear of the natural man, it has ever been sweet to the ear of faith. Millions have been morally and spiritually transformed by this message, have lived lives of great moral power, and died at last peacefully trusting in it.

This message of justice discharged and mercy operative is more than a pleasant theological theory; it announces a fact made necessary by our deep human need. Because of our sin we are all under sentence of death, a judgment which resulted when justice confronted our moral situation. When infinite equity encountered our chronic and willful in-equity, there was violent war between the two, a war which God won and must always win. But when the penitent sinner casts himself upon Christ for salvation, the moral situation is reversed. Justice confronts the changed situation and pronounces the believing man just. Thus justice actually goes over to the side of God's trusting children. This is the meaning of those daring words of the apostle John: "If we confess our sins, he is faithful and just to forgive us our sins, and to cleanse us from all unrighteousness."

But God's justice stands forever against the sinner in utter severity. The vague and tenuous hope that God is too kind to punish the ungodly has become a deadly opiate for the consciences of millions. It hushes their fears and allows them to practice all pleasant forms of iniquity while death draws every day nearer and the command to repent goes unregarded. As responsible moral beings we dare not so trifle with our eternal future.

> *Jesus, Thy blood and righteousness*
> *My beauty are, my glorious dress;*
> *'Midst flaming worlds, in these arrayed,*
> *With joy shall I lift up my head.*
>
> *Bold shall I stand in Thy great day;*
> *For who aught to my charge shall lay?*
> *Fully absolved through these I am—*
> *From sin and fear, from guilt and shame.*
>
> Count N. L. von Zinzendorf

3

The Mercy of God

Holy Father, Thy wisdom excites our admiration, Thy power fills us with fear, Thy omnipresence turns every spot of earth into holy ground; but how shall we thank Thee enough for Thy mercy which comes down to the lowest part of our need to give us beauty for ashes, the oil of joy for mourning, and for the spirit of heaviness a garment of praise? We bless and magnify Thy mercy, through Jesus Christ our Lord. Amen.

When through the blood of the everlasting covenant we children of the shadows reach at last our home in the light, we shall have a thousand strings to our harps, but the sweetest may well be the one tuned to sound forth most perfectly the mercy of God.

For what right will we have to be there? Did we not by our sins take part in that unholy rebellion which rashly sought to dethrone the glorious King of creation? And did we not in times past walk according to the course of this world, according to the evil prince of the power of the air, the spirit that now works in the sons of disobedience? And did we not all once live in the lusts of our flesh? And were we not by nature the children of wrath, even as others? But we who were one time enemies and alienated in our minds through wicked works shall then see God face to face and His name shall be on our foreheads. We who earned banishment shall enjoy communion; we who deserve the pains

25

of hell shall know the bliss of heaven. And all through
the tender mercy of our God, whereby the Dayspring
from on high hath visited us.

> *When all Thy mercies, O my God,*
>   *My rising soul surveys,*
> *Transported with the view, I'm lost*
>   *In wonder, love, and praise.*
>
> Joseph Addison

Mercy is an attribute of God, an infinite and inexhaust-
ible energy within the divine nature which disposes God to
be actively compassionate. Both the Old and the New Tes-
taments proclaim the mercy of God, but the Old has more
than four times as much to say about it as the New.

We should banish from our minds forever the common
but erroneous notion that justice and judgment charac-
terize the God of Israel, while mercy and grace belong to
the Lord of the Church. Actually there is in principle no
difference between the Old Testament and the New. In the
New Testament Scriptures there is a fuller development of
redemptive truth, but one God speaks in both dispensations, and what He speaks agrees with what He is.
Wherever and whenever God appears to men, He acts like
Himself. Whether in the Garden of Eden or the Garden of
Gethsemane, God is merciful as well as just. He has always dealt in mercy with mankind and will always deal in
justice when His mercy is despised. Thus He did in an-
tediluvian times; thus when Christ walked among men;
thus He is doing today and will continue always to do for
no other reason than that He is God.

If we could remember that the divine mercy is not a
temporary mood but an attribute of God's eternal being,
we would no longer fear that it will someday cease to be.
Mercy never began to be, but from eternity was; so it will
never cease to be. It will never be more since it is in itself
infinite; and it will never be less because the infinite cannot
suffer diminution. Nothing that has occurred or will occur

in heaven or earth or hell can change the tender mercies of our God. Forever His mercy stands, a boundless, overwhelming immensity of divine pity and compassion.

As judgment is God's justice confronting moral inequity, so mercy is the goodness of God confronting human suffering and guilt. Were there no guilt in the world, no pain and no tears, God would yet be infinitely merciful; but His mercy might well remain hidden in His heart, unknown to the created universe. No voice would be raised to celebrate the mercy of which none felt the need. It is human misery and sin that call forth the divine mercy.

"Kyrie eleison! Christe eleison!" the Church has pleaded through the centuries; but if I mistake not I hear in the voice of her pleading a note of sadness and despair. Her plaintive cry, so often repeated in that tone of resigned dejection, compels one to infer that she is praying for a boon she never actually expects to receive. She may go on dutifully to sing of the greatness of God and to recite the creed times beyond number, but her plea for mercy sounds like a forlorn hope and no more, as if mercy were a heavenly gift to be longed for but never really enjoyed.

Could our failure to capture the pure joy of mercy consciously experienced be the result of our unbelief or our ignorance, or both? It was so once in Israel. "I bear them record," Paul testified of Israel, "that they have a zeal of God, but not according to knowledge." They failed because there was at least one thing they did not know, one thing that would have made the difference. And of Israel in the wilderness the Hebrew writer says, "But the word preached did not profit them, not being mixed with faith in them that heard it." To receive mercy we must first know that God is merciful. And it is not enough to believe that He once showed mercy to Noah or Abraham or David and will again show mercy in some happy future day. We must believe that God's mercy is boundless, free and, through Jesus Christ our Lord, available to us now in our present situation.

We may plead for mercy for a lifetime in unbelief, and at the end of our days be still no more than sadly hopeful that we shall somewhere, sometime, receive it. This is to starve to death just outside the banquet hall into which we have been warmly invited. Or we may, if we will, lay hold on the mercy of God by faith, enter the hall, and sit down with the bold and avid souls who will not allow diffidence and unbelief to keep them from the feast of fat things prepared for them.

> *Arise, my soul, arise;*
> *Shake off thy guilty fears;*
> *The bleeding Sacrifice*
> *In my behalf appears:*
> *Before the throne my Surety stands,*
> *My name is written on His Hands.*
>
> *My God is reconciled;*
> *His pardoning voice I hear:*
> *He owns me for His child;*
> *I can no longer fear:*
> *With confidence I now draw nigh*
> *And "Father, Abba, Father," cry.*

Charles Wesley

4

The Sovereignty of God

Who wouldst not fear Thee, O Lord God of Hosts, most high and most terrible? For Thou art Lord alone. Thou hast made heaven and the heaven of heavens, the earth and all things that are therein, and in Thy hand is the soul of every living thing. Thou sittest king upon the flood; yea, Thou sittest king forever. Thou art a great king over all the the earth. Thou art clothed with strength; honor and majesty are before Thee. Amen.

God's sovereignty is the attribute by which He rules His entire creation, and to be sovereign God must be all-knowing, all-powerful, and absolutely free. The reasons are these:

Were there even one datum of knowledge, however small, unknown to God, His rule would break down at that point. To be Lord over all the creation, He must possess all knowledge. And were God lacking one infinitesimal modicum of power, that lack would end His reign and undo His kingdom; that one stray atom of power would belong to someone else and God would be a limited ruler and hence not sovereign.

Furthermore, His sovereignty requires that He be absolutely free, which means simply that He must be free to do whatever He wills to do anywhere at any time to carry out His eternal purpose in every single detail without interference. Were He less than free He must be less than sovereign.

To grasp the idea of unqualified freedom requires a vigorous effort of the mind. We are not psychologically conditioned to understand freedom except in its imperfect forms. Our concepts of it have been shaped in a world where no absolute freedom exists. Here each natural object is dependent upon many other objects, and that dependence limits its freedom.

Wordsworth at the beginning of his "Prelude" rejoiced that he had escaped the city where he had long been pent up and was "now free, free as a bird to settle where I will." But to be free as a bird is not to be free at all. The naturalist knows that the supposedly free bird actually lives its entire life in a cage made of fears, hungers, and instincts; it is limited by weather conditions, varying air pressures, the local food supply, predatory beasts, and that strangest of all bonds, the irresistible compulsion to stay within the small plot of land and air assigned it by birdland comity. The freest bird is, along with every other created thing, held in constant check by a net of necessity. Only God is free.

God is said to be absolutely free because no one and no thing can hinder Him or compel Him or stop Him. He is able to do as He pleases always, everywhere, forever. To be thus free means also that He must possess universal authority. That He has unlimited power we know from the Scriptures and may deduce from certain other of His attributes. But what about His authority?

Even to discuss the authority of Almighty God seems a bit meaningless, and to question it would be absurd. Can we imagine the Lord God of Hosts having to request permission of anyone or to apply for anything to a higher body? To whom would God go for permission? Who is higher than the Highest? Who is mightier than the Almighty? Whose position antedates that of the Eternal? At whose throne would God kneel? Where is the greater one to whom He must appeal? "Thus saith the Lord the King of Israel, and his redeemer the Lord of hosts; I am the first, and I am the last; and beside me there is no God."

The sovereignty of God is a fact well established in the Scriptures and declared aloud by the logic of truth. But admittedly it raises certain problems which have not to this time been satisfactorily solved. These are mainly two.

The first is the presence in the creation of those things which God cannot approve, such as evil, pain, and death. If God is sovereign He could have prevented their coming into existence. Why did He not do so?

The *Zend-Avesta,* sacred book of Zoroastrianism, loftiest of the great non-Biblical religions, got around this difficulty neatly enough by postulating a theological dualism. There were two Gods, Ormazd and Ahriman, and these between them created the world. The good Ormazd made all good things and the evil Ahriman made the rest. It was quite simple. Ormazd had no sovereignty to worry about, and apparently did not mind sharing his prerogatives with another.

For the Christian this explanation will not do, for it flatly contradicts the truth taught so emphatically throughout the whole Bible, that there is one God and that He alone created the heaven and the earth and all the things that are therein. God's attributes are such as to make impossible the existence of another God. The Christian admits that he does not have the final answer to the riddle of permitted evil. But he knows what that answer is not. And he knows that the *Zend-Avesta* does not have it either.

While a complete explanation of the origin of sin eludes us, there are a few things we do know. In His sovereign wisdom God has permitted evil to exist in carefully restricted areas of His creation, a kind of fugitive outlaw whose activities are temporary and limited in scope. In doing this God has acted according to His infinite wisdom and goodness. More than that no one knows at present; and more than that no one needs to know. The name of God is sufficient guarantee of the perfection of His works.

Another real problem created by the doctrine of the divine sovereignty has to do with the will of man. If God rules His universe by His sovereign decrees, how is it possible for man to exercise free choice? And if he cannot exercise freedom of choice, how can he be held responsible for his conduct? Is he not a mere puppet whose actions are determined by a behind-the-scenes God who pulls the strings as it pleases Him?

The attempt to answer these questions has divided the Christian church neatly into two camps which have borne the names of two distinguished theologians, Jacobus Arminius and John Calvin. Most Christians are content to get into one camp or the other and deny either sovereignty to God or free will to man. It appears possible, however, to reconcile these two positions without doing violence to either, although the effort that follows may prove deficient to partisans of one camp or the other.

Here is my view: God sovereignly decreed that man should be free to exercise moral choice, and man from the beginning has fulfilled that decree by making his choice between good and evil. When he chooses to do evil, he does not thereby countervail the sovereign will of God but fulfills it, inasmuch as the eternal decree decided not which choice the man should make but that he should be free to make it. If in His absolute freedom God has willed to give man limited freedom, who is there to stay His hand or say, "What doest thou?" Man's will is free because God is sovereign. A God less than sovereign could not bestow moral freedom upon His creatures. He would be afraid to do so.

Perhaps a homely illustration might help us to understand. An ocean liner leaves New York bound for Liverpool. Its destination has been determined by proper authorities. Nothing can change it. This is at least a faint picture of sovereignty.

On board the liner are several scores of passengers. These are not in chains, neither are their activities determined for them by decree. They are completely free to move about as they will. They eat, sleep, play, lounge about on the deck, read, talk, altogether as they please; but all the while the great liner is carrying them steadily onward toward a predetermined port.

Both freedom and sovereignty are present here and they do not contradict each other. So it is, I believe, with man's freedom and the sovereignty of God. The mighty liner of God's sovereign design keeps its steady course over the sea of history. God moves undisturbed and unhindered toward the fulfillment of those eternal purposes which He purposed in Christ Jesus before the world began. We do not know all that is included in those purposes, but enough has been disclosed to furnish us with a broad outline of things to come and to give us good hope and firm assurance of future well-being.

We know that God will fulfill every promise made to the prophets; we know that sinners will some day be cleansed out of the earth; we know that a ransomed company will enter into the joy of God and that the righteous will shine forth in the kingdom of their Father; we know that God's perfections will yet receive universal acclamation, that all created intelligences will own Jesus Christ Lord to the glory of God the Father, that the present imperfect order will be done away, and a new heaven and a new earth be established forever.

Toward all this God is moving with infinite wisdom and perfect precision of action. No one can dissuade Him from His purposes; nothing turn Him aside from His plans. Since He is omniscient, there can be no unforeseen circumstances, no accidents. As He is sovereign, there can be no countermanded orders, no breakdown in authority; and as He is omnipotent, there can be no want of power to achieve His chosen ends. God is sufficient unto Himself for all these things.

In the meanwhile things are not as smooth as this quick outline might suggest. The mystery of iniquity doth already work. Within the broad field of God's sovereign, permissive will the deadly conflict of good with evil continues with increasing fury. God will yet have His way in the whirlwind and the storm, but the storm and the whirlwind are here, and as responsible beings we must make our choice in the present moral situation.

Certain things have been decreed by the free determination of God, and one of these is the law of choice and consequences. God has decreed that all who willingly commit themselves to His Son Jesus Christ in the obedience of faith shall receive eternal life and become sons of God. He has also decreed that all who love darkness and continue in rebellion against the high authority of heaven shall remain in a state of spiritual alienation and suffer eternal death at last.

Reducing the whole matter to individual terms, we arrive at some vital and highly personal conclusions. In the moral conflict now raging around us whoever is on God's side is on the winning side and cannot lose; whoever is on the other side is on the losing side and cannot win. Here there is no chance, no gamble. There is freedom to choose which side we shall be on but no freedom to negotiate the results of the choice once it is made. By the mercy of God we may repent a wrong choice and alter the consequences by making a new and right choice. Beyond that we cannot go.

The whole matter of moral choice centers around Jesus Christ. Christ stated it plainly: "He that is not with me is against me," and "No man cometh unto the Father, but by me." The gospel message embodies three distinct elements: an announcement, a command, and a call. It announces the good news of redemption accomplished in mercy; it commands all men everywhere to repent and it calls all men to surrender to the terms of grace by believing on Jesus Christ as Lord and Saviour.

We must all choose whether we will obey the gospel or turn away in unbelief and reject its authority. Our choice is our own, but the consequences of the choice have already been determined by the sovereign will of God, and from this there is no appeal.

The Lord descended from above,
  And bowed the heavens most high,
And underneath His feet He cast
  The darkness of the sky.

On cherubim and seraphim
  Full royally He rode,
And on the wings of mighty winds
  Came flying all abroad.

He sat serene upon the floods,
  Their fury to restrain;
And He, as sovereign Lord and King,
  For evermore shall reign.

Psalm paraphrase,
by Thomas Sternhold

Excerpts from
The Divine Conquest

5

The Forgotten One

The comforter, which is the Holy Ghost.
John 14:26

In neglecting or denying the deity of Christ the Liberals have committed a tragic blunder, for it leaves them nothing but an imperfect Christ whose death was a mere martyrdom and whose resurrection is a myth. They who follow a merely human Saviour follow no Saviour at all, but an ideal only, and one furthermore that can do no more than mock their weaknesses and sins. If Mary's son was not the Son of God in a sense no other man is, then there can be no more hope for the human race. If He who called Himself the Light of the World was only a flickering torch, then the darkness that enshrouds the earth is here to stay. So-called Christian leaders shrug this off, but their responsibility toward the souls of their flocks cannot be dismissed with a shrug. God will yet bring them to account for the injury they have done to the plain people who trusted them as spiritual guides.

But however culpable the act of the Liberal in denying the Godhood of Christ, we who pride ourselves on our orthodoxy must not allow our indignation to blind us to our own shortcomings. Certainly this is no time for self-congratulations, for we too have in recent years committed a costly blunder in religion, a blunder paralleling closely that of the Liberal. Our blunder (or shall we frankly say our sin?) has been to neglect the doctrine of the Spirit to a point where we virtually deny Him His place in the Godhead. This denial has not been by open doctrinal statement, for we have clung closely enough to the Biblical position wherever our credal pronouncements are concerned. Our formal creed is sound; *the breakdown is in our working creed.*

This is not a trifling distinction. A doctrine has practical value only as far as it is *prominent in our thoughts* and *makes a difference in our lives.* By this test the doctrine of the Holy Spirit as held by evangelical Christians today has almost no practical value at all. In most Christian churches the Spirit is quite entirely overlooked. Whether He is present or absent makes no real difference to anyone. Brief reference is made to Him in the Doxology and the Benediction. Further than that He might as well not exist. So completely do we ignore Him that it is only by courtesy that we can be called Trinitarian. The Christian doctrine of the Trinity boldly declares the equality of the Three Persons and the right of the Holy Spirit to be worshipped and glorified. Anything less than this is something less than Trinitarianism.

Our neglect of the doctrine of the blessed Third Person has had and is having serious consequences. For doctrine is dynamite. It must have emphasis sufficiently sharp to detonate it before its power is released. Failing this it may lie quiescent in the back of our minds for the whole of our lives without effect. The doctrine of the Spirit is buried dynamite. Its power awaits discovery and use by the Church. The power of the Spirit will not be given to any mincing assent to pneumatological truth. The Holy Spirit cares not at all whether we write Him into our credenda in the back of our hymnals; He waits for our *emphasis.* When He gets into the thinking of the teachers He will get into the expectation of the hearers. When the Holy Spirit ceases to be incidental and again becomes fundamental the power of the Spirit will be asserted once more among the people called Christians.

The idea of the Spirit held by the average church member is so vague as to be nearly nonexistent. When he thinks of the matter at all he is likely to try to imagine a nebulous substance like a wisp of invisible smoke which is said to be present in churches and to hover over good people when they are dying. Frankly he does not believe in any such thing, but he wants to believe something, and not feeling up to the task of examining the whole truth in the light of Scripture he compromises by holding belief in the Spirit as far out from the center of his life as possible, letting it make no difference in anything that touches him practically. This describes a surprisingly large number of earnest persons who are sincerely trying to be Christians.

Now, how should we think of the Spirit? A full answer might well run to a dozen volumes. We can at best only point to the "gracious Unction from above" and hope that the reader's own desire may provide the necessary stimulus to urge him on to know the blessed Third Person for himself.

If I read aright the record of Christian experience through the years, those who most enjoyed the power of the Spirit have had the least to say about Him by way of attempted definition. The Bible saint who walked in the Spirit never tried to explain Him. In post-Biblical times many who were filled and possessed by the Spirit were by the limitations of their literary gifts prevented from telling us much about Him. They had no gift for self-analysis, but lived from within in uncritical simplicity. To them the Spirit was One to be loved and fellowshipped the same as the Lord Jesus Himself. They would have been lost completely in any metaphysical discussion of the nature of the Spirit, but they had no trouble in claiming the power of the Spirit for holy living and fruitful service.

This is as it should be. Personal experience must always be first in real life. The most important thing is that we experience reality by the shortest and most direct method. A child may eat nutritious food without knowing anything

about chemistry or diatetics. A country boy may know the
delights of pure love while never having heard of Sigmund
Freud or Havelock Ellis. Knowledge by acquaintance is always better than mere knowledge by description, and the
first does not presuppose the second nor require it.

In religion more than in any other field of human experience a sharp distinction must always be made between
knowing about and *knowing*. The distinction is the same as
between knowing about food and actually eating it. A man
can die of starvation knowing all about bread, and a man
can remain spiritually dead while knowing all the historic
facts of Christianity. "This is life eternal, that they might
know thee the only true God, and Jesus Christ, whom
thou has sent." We have but to introduce one extra word
into this verse to see how vast is the difference between
knowing about and knowing. "This is life eternal, that they
might know *about* thee the only true God, and Jesus
Christ, whom thou has sent." That one word makes all the
difference between life and death, for it goes to the very
root of the verse and changes its theology radically and
vitally.

For all this we would not underestimate the importance
of mere knowing about. Its value lies in its ability to rouse
us to desire to know in actual experience. Thus knowledge
by description may lead on to knowledge by acquaintance.
May lead on, I say, but does not necessarily do so. Thus we
dare not conclude that because we learn about the Spirit
we for that reason actually know Him. Knowing Him
comes only by a personal encounter with the Holy Spirit
himself.

How shall we think of the Spirit? A great deal can be
learned about the Holy Spirit from the word *spirit* itself.
Spirit means existence on a level above and beyond matter;
it means life subsisting in another mode. Spirit is substance
that has no weight, no dimension, no size nor extension in
space. These qualities belong to matter and can have no
application to spirit. Yet spirit has true being and is objec-

tively real. If this is hard to visualize, just pass it up, for it is at best but a clumsy attempt of the mind to grasp that which is above the mind's powers. And no harm is done if in our thinking about the Spirit we are forced by the limitations of our intellects to clothe Him in the familiar habiliments of material form.

How shall we think of the Spirit? The Bible and Christian theology agree to teach that He is a Person, endowed with every quality of personality, such as emotion, intellect and will. He knows, He wills, He loves; He feels affection, antipathy and compassion. He thinks, sees, hears and speaks and performs any act of which personality is capable.

One quality belonging to the Holy Spirit, of great interest and importance to every seeking heart, is penetrability. He can penetrate matter, such as the human body; He can penetrate mind; He can penetrate another spirit, such as the human spirit. He can achieve complete penetration of and actual intermingling with the human spirit. He can invade the human heart and make room for Himself without expelling anything essentially human. The integrity of the human personality remains unimpaired. Only moral evil is forced to withdraw.

The metaphysical problem involved here can no more be avoided than it can be solved. How can one personality enter another? The candid reply would be simply that we do not know, but a near approach to an understanding may be made by a simple analogy borrowed from the old devotional writers of several hundred years ago. We place a piece of iron in a fire and blow up the coals. At first we have two distinct substances, iron and fire. When we insert the iron in the fire we achieve the penetration of the fire by the iron. Soon the fire begins to penetrate the iron and we have not only the iron in the fire but the fire in the iron as well. They are two distinct substances, but they have comingled and interpenetrated to a point where the two have become one.

In some such manner does the Holy Spirit penetrate our spirits. In the whole experience we remain our very selves. There is no destruction of substance. Each remains a separate being as before; the difference is that now the Spirit penetrates and fills our personalities and we are *experientially one with God.*

How shall we think of the Holy Spirit? The Bible declares that He is God. Every quality belonging to Almighty God is freely attributed to Him. All that God is, the Spirit is declared to be. The Spirit of God is one with and equal to God just as the spirit of a man is equal to and one with the man. This is so fully taught in the Scriptures that we may without loss to the argument omit the formality of proof texts. The most casual reader will have discovered it for himself.

The historic Church when she formulated her "rule of faith" boldly wrote into her confession her belief in the Godhood of the Holy Ghost. The Apostles' Creed witnesses to faith in the Father and in the Son and in the Holy Ghost, and makes no difference between the Three. The Fathers who composed the Nicene Creed testified in a passage of great beauty to their faith in the deity of the Spirit:

> *And I believe in the Holy Ghost,*
> *The Lord and Giver of Life,*
> *Who proceedeth from the Father and the Son;*
> *Who with the Father and Son together*
> *Is worshipped and glorified.*

The Arian controversy of the Fourth Century compelled the Fathers to state their beliefs with greater clarity than before. Among the important writings which appeared at that time is the Athanasian Creed. Who composed it matters little to us now. It was written as an attempt to state in as few words as possible what the Bible teaches about the nature of God; and this it has done with a comprehensiveness and precision hardly matched anywhere in the literature of the world. Here are a few quotations bearing on the deity of the Holy Ghost:

"There is one Person of the Father, another of the Son: and another of the Holy Ghost.

But the Godhead of the Father, of the Son, and of the Holy Ghost, is all one: the Glory equal, the Majesty co-eternal.

And in this Trinity none is afore, or after other: none is greater, or less than another;

But the whole three Persons are co-eternal together: and co-equal.

So that in all things, as is aforesaid: the Unity in Trinity, and Trinity in Unity is to be worshipped."

In her sacred hymnody the Church has freely acknowl-edged the Godhead of the Spirit and in her inspired song she has worshipped Him with joyous abandon. Some of our hymns to the Spirit have become so familiar that we tend to miss their true meaning by the very circumstance of their familiarity. Such a hymn is the wondrous "Holy Ghost, With Light Divine"; another is the more recent "Breathe on Me, Breath of God"; and there are many oth-ers. They have been sung so often by persons who have had no experiential knowledge of their content, that for the most of us they have become almost meaningless.

In the poetical works of Frederick Faber I have found a hymn to the Holy Spirit which I would rank among the finest ever written, but so far as I know it has not been set to music, or if it has, it is not sung today in any church with which I am acquainted. Could the reason be that it em-bodies personal experience of the Holy Spirit so deep, so intimate, so fiery hot that it corresponds to nothing in the hearts of the worshippers in present-day evangelicalism? I quote three stanzas:

> *Fountain of Love! Thyself true God!*
> *Who through eternal days*
> *From Father and from Son hast flowed*
> *In uncreated ways!*

I dread Thee, Unbegotten Love!
  True God! sole Fount of Grace!
And now before Thy blessed throne
  My sinful self abase.

O Light! O Love! O very God
  I dare no longer gaze
Upon Thy wondrous attributes
  And their mysterious ways.

These lines have everything to make a great hymn, sound theology, smooth structure, lyric beauty, high compression of profound ideas and a full charge of lofty religious feeling. Yet they are in complete neglect. I believe that a mighty resurgence of the Spirit's power among us will open again wells of hymnody long forgotten. For song can never bring the Holy Spirit, but the Holy Spirit does invariably bring song.

What we have in the Christian doctrine of the Holy Spirit is Deity present among us. He is not God's messenger only, *He is God.* He is God in contact with His creatures, doing in them and among them a saving and renewing work.

The Persons of the Godhead never work separately. We dare not think of them in such a way as to "divide the substance." Every act of God is done by all three Persons. God is never anywhere present in one Person without the other two. He cannot divide Himself. Where the Spirit is, there also is the Father and the Son. "We will come unto him and make our abode with him." For the accomplishment of some specific work one Person may for the time be more prominent than the others are, but never is He alone. God is altogether present wherever He is present at all.

To the reverent question, "What is God like?" a proper answer will always be, "He is like Christ." For Christ is God, and the Man who walked among men in Palestine was God acting like Himself in the familiar situation where

His incarnation placed Him. To the question, "What is the Spirit like?" the answer must always be, "He is like Christ." For the Spirit is the essence of the Father and the Son. As they are, so is He. As we feel toward Christ and toward our Father who art in heaven, so should we feel toward the Spirit of the Father and the Son.

The Holy Spirit is the Spirit of life and light and love. In His uncreated nature He is a boundless sea of fire, flowing, moving ever, performing as He moves the eternal purposes of God. Toward nature He performs one sort of work, toward the world another and toward the Church still another. And every act of His accords with the will of the Triune God. Never does He act on impulse nor move after a quick or arbitrary decision. Since He is the Spirit of the Father He feels toward His people exactly as the Father feels, so there need be on our part no sense of strangeness in His presence. He will always act like Jesus, toward sinners in compassion, toward saints in warm affection, toward human suffering in tenderest pity and love.

It is time for us to repent, for our transgressions against the blessed Third Person have been many and much aggravated. We have bitterly mistreated Him in the House of His friends. We have crucified Him in His own temple as they crucified the Eternal Son on the hill above Jerusalem. And the nails we used were not of iron, but of the finer and more precious stuff of which human life is made. Out of our hearts we took the refined metals of will and feeling and thought, and from them we fashioned the nails of suspicion and rebellion and neglect. By unworthy thoughts about Him and unfriendly attitudes toward Him we grieved and quenched Him days without end.

The truest and most acceptable repentance is to reverse the acts and attitudes of which we repent. A thousand years of remorse over a wrong act would not please God as much as a change of conduct and a reformed life. "Let the wicked forsake his way, and the unrighteous man his thoughts: and let him return unto the Lord, and he will have mercy upon him; and to our God , for he will abundantly pardon."

We can best repent our neglect by neglecting Him no more. Let us begin to think of Him as One to be worshipped and obeyed. Let us throw open every door and invite Him in. Let us surrender to Him every room in the temple of our hearts and insist that He enter and occupy as Lord and Master within His own dwelling. And let us remember that He is drawn to the sweet Name of Jesus as bees are drawn to the fragrance of clover. Where Christ is glorified He will move about freely, pleased and at home.

6

The Illumination of the Spirit

*John answered and said, A man can receive
nothing except it be given him from Heaven.*

John 3:27

Here in a brief sentence is the hope and despair of mankind. "A man can receive nothing." From the context we know that John is speaking of spiritual truth. He is telling us that there is a kind of truth which can never be grasped by the intellect, for the intellect exists for the apprehension of ideas, and this truth consists not in ideas but in life. Divine truth is of the nature of spirit and for that reason can be received only by spiritual revelation. "Except it be given him from heaven."

This was no new doctrine which John here set forth, but an advance rather upon truth already taught in the Old Testament. The prophet Isaiah, for instance, has this passage, "My thoughts are not your thoughts, neither are my ways your ways, saith the Lord. For as the heavens are higher than the earth, so are my ways higher than your ways, and my thoughts than your thoughts." Perhaps this had meant to its readers no more than that God's thoughts, while similar to ours, were loftier, and His ways as high above ours as would befit the ways of One whose wisdom is infinite and whose power is without bounds. Now John says plainly enough that God's thoughts are not

49

only greater than ours quantitatively but qualitatively wholly different from ours. God's thoughts belong to the world of spirit, man's to the world of intellect, and while spirit can embrace intellect, the human intellect can never comprehend spirit. Man's thoughts cannot cross over into God's. "How unsearchable are his judgments, and his ways past finding out!"

God made man in His own image and placed within him an organ by means of which he could know spiritual things. When man sinned that organ died. "Dead in sin" is a description not of the body nor yet of the intellect, but of the organ of God-knowledge within the human soul. Now men are forced to depend upon another and inferior organ and one furthermore which is wholly inadequate to the purpose. I mean, of course, the mind as the seat of his powers of reason and understanding.

Man by reason cannot know God; he can only *know about* God. Through the light of reason certain important facts about God may be discovered. "Because that which may be known of God is manifest in them; for God hath showed it unto them. For the invisible things of him from the creation of the world are clearly seen, being understood by the things which are made, even his eternal power and Godhead; so that they are without excuse." Through the light of nature man's moral reason may be enlightened, but the deeper mysteries of God remain hidden to him until he has received illumination from above. "But the natural man receiveth not the things of the Spirit of God: for they are foolishness unto him: neither can he know them, because they are spiritually discerned." When the Spirit illuminates the heart, then a part of the man sees which never saw before; a part of him knows which never knew before, and that with a kind of knowing which the most acute thinker cannot imitate. He knows now in a deep and authoritative way, and what he knows needs no reasoned proof. His experience of knowing is above rea-

son, immediate, perfectly convincing and inwardly satisfying.

"A man can receive nothing." That is the burden of the
Bible. Whatever men may think of human reason God
takes a low view of it. "Where is the wise? where is the
scribe? where is the disputer of the world? hath not God
made foolish the wisdom of this world?" Man's reason is a
fine instrument and useful within its field. It is a gift of
God and God does not hesitate to appeal to it, as when He
cries to Israel, "Come now, and let us reason together."
The inability of human reason as an organ of divine knowledge arises not from its own weakness but from its unfit-
tedness for the task by its own nature. It was not given as
an organ by which to know God.

The doctrine of the inability of the human mind and the
need for divine illumination is so fully developed in the
New Testament that it is nothing short of astonishing that
we should have gone so far astray about the whole thing.
Fundamentalism has stood aloof from the Liberal in self-
conscious superiority and has on its own part fallen into
error, the error of textualism, which is simply orthodoxy
without the Holy Ghost. Everywhere among Conserva-
tives we find persons who are Bible-taught but not Spirit-
taught. They conceive truth to be something which they
can grasp with the mind. If a man hold to the fundamen-
tals of the Christian faith he is thought to possess divine
truth. But it does not follow. There is no truth apart from
the Spirit. The most brilliant intellect may be imbecilic
when confronted with the mysteries of God. For a man to
understand revealed truth requires an act of God equal to
the original act which inspired the text.

"Except it be given him from heaven." Here is the other
side of the truth; here is hope for all, for these words do
certainly mean that there is such a thing as a gift of knowing, a gift that comes from heaven. Christ taught His disciples to expect the coming of the Spirit of Truth who would

teach them all things. He explained Peter's knowledge of His Saviourhood as being a direct revelation from the Father in heaven. And in one of His prayers He said, "I thank thee, O Father, Lord of heaven and earth, because thou hast hidden these things from the wise and prudent, and hast revealed them unto babes." By "the wise and prudent" our Lord meant not Greek philosophers but Jewish Bible students and teachers of the Law.

This basic idea, the inability of human reason as an instrument of God-knowledge, was fully developed in the epistles of Paul. The Apostle frankly rules out every natural faculty as instruments for discovering divine truth and throws us back helpless upon the inworking Spirit. "Eye hath not seen, nor ear heard, neither hath entered into the heart of man, the things which God hath prepared for them that love him. For God hath revealed them unto us by his Spirit: for the Spirit searcheth all things, yea, the deep things of God. For what man knoweth the things of a man, save the spirit of man which is in him? even so the things of God knoweth no man, but the Spirit of God. Now we have received, not the Spirit of the world, but the Spirit which is of God; that we might know the things which are freely given to us of God."

The passage just quoted is taken from Paul's First Epistle to the Corinthians and is not lifted out of context nor placed in a setting which would tend to distort its meaning. Indeed it expresses the very essence of Paul's spiritual philosophy and fully accords with the rest of the Epistle, and I might add, with the rest of Paul's writings as we have them preserved in the New Testament. That type of theological rationalism which is so popular today would have been wholly foreign to the mind of the great Apostle. He had not faith in man's ability to comprehend truth apart from the direct illumination of the Holy Ghost.

I have just now used the word *rationalism* and I must either retract it or justify its use in association with orthodoxy. The latter I think I shall have no trouble doing.

For the textualism of our times is based upon the same premise as the old-line rationalism, that is, the belief that the human mind is the supreme authority in the judgment of truth. Or otherwise stated, it is *confidence in the ability of the human mind to do that which the Bible declares it was never created to do and consequently is wholly incapable of doing.* Philosophical rationalism is honest enough to reject the Bible flatly. Theological rationalism rejects it while pretending to accept it and in so doing puts out its own eyes.

The inward kernel of truth has the same configuration as the outward shell. The mind can grasp the shell but only the Spirit of God can lay hold of the internal essence. Our great error has been that we have trusted to the shell and have believed we were sound in the faith because we were able to explain the external shape of truth as found in the letter of the Word. From this mortal error Fundamentalism is slowly dying. We have forgotten that the essence of spiritual truth cannot come to the one who knows the external shell of truth unless there is first a miraculous operation of the Spirit within the heart. Those overtones of religious delight which accompany truth when the Spirit illuminates it are all but missing from the Church today. Those transporting glimpses of the Celestial Country are few and dim; the fragrance of "Sharon's dewy Rose" is hardly discernible. Consequently we have been forced to look elsewhere for our delights and we have found them in the dubious artistry of converted opera singers or the tinkling melodies of odd and curious musical arrangements. We have tried to secure spiritual pleasures by working upon fleshly emotions and whipping up synthetic feeling by means wholly carnal. And the total effect has been evil.

In a remarkable sermon on "The True Way of Attaining Divine Knowledge," John Smith states the truth I am attempting to set forth here. "Were I indeed to define divinity I should rather call it a divine *life* than a divine *science;* it is something rather to be understood by a *spiritual sensation,* than by any *verbal description.* . . . Divinity is indeed a true *efflux* from the eternal Light, which like the sunbeams, does not only enlighten, but *heat* and *enliven*.... We must not think that we have attained to the right knowledge of truth, when we have broken through the outward shell of words and phrases that house it up;... There is a knowing of Truth as it is in Jesus, as it is in a Christ-like nature, as it is in that sweet, mild, humble, and loving Spirit of Jesus, which spreads itself like a morning sun upon the souls of good men, full of life and light. It profits little to know Christ Himself after the flesh; but he gives his Spirit to good men that search the deep things of God. There is an inward beauty, life and loveliness in divine Truth, which can be known only when it is digested into life and practice."

This old Divine held that a pure life was absolutely necessary to any real understanding of spiritual truth. "There is," he says, "an inward sweetness and deliciousness in divine truth, which no sensual mind can taste or relish: this is that 'natural' man that savors not the things of God... Divinity is not so much perceived by a subtle wit as by a purified sense."

Twelve hundred years before these words were uttered Athanasius had written a profound treatise called, "The Incarnation of the Word of God." In this treatise he boldly attacked the difficult problems inherent in the doctrine of the Incarnation. The whole thing is a remarkable demonstration of pure reason engaged with divine relevation. He makes a great case for the deity of Christ, and for all who believe the Bible, settles the matter for all time. Yet so little does he trust the human mind to comprehend divine mysteries that he closes his great work with a strong warning against a mere intellectual understanding of spiritual truth. His words should be printed in large type and tacked on the desk of every pastor and theological student in the world:

"But for the searching of the Scriptures and true knowledge of them, an honorable life is needed, and a pure soul, and that virtue which is according to Christ; so that the intellect guiding its path by it, may be able to attain what it desires, and to comprehend it, in so far as it is accessible to human nature to learn concerning the word of God. For without a pure mind and a modeling of the life after the saints, a man could not possibly comprehend the words of the saints.... He that would comprehend the mind of those who speak of God needs begin by washing and cleansing his soul."

The old Jewish believers of pre-Christian times who gave us the (to modern Protestants little-known) books, the Wisdom of Solomon and Ecclesiasticus, believed that it is impossible for an impure heart to know divine truth. "For into a malicious soul wisdom will not enter; nor dwell in the body that is subject unto sin. For the holy spirit of discipline will flee deceit, and remove from thoughts that are without understanding, and will not abide when unrighteousness cometh in."

These books, along with our familiar Book of Proverbs, teach that true spiritual knowledge is the result of a visitation of heavenly wisdom, a kind of baptism of the Spirit of Truth which comes to God-fearing men. This wisdom is always associated with righteousness and humility and is never found apart from godliness and true holiness of life.

Conservative Christians in this day are stumbling over this truth. We need to re-examine the whole thing. We need to learn that truth consists not in correct doctrine, but in correct doctrine *plus the inward enlightenment of the Holy Spirit*. We must declare again the mystery of wisdom from above. A re-preachment of this vital truth could result in a fresh breath from God upon a stale and suffocating orthodoxy.

7

The Spirit as Power

> *But ye shall receive power, after that*
> *The Holy Ghost is come upon you. . . .*
>
> Acts 1:8

Some good Christians have misread this text and have assumed that Christ told his disciples that they were to receive the Holy Spirit *and* power, the power to come after the coming of the Spirit. A superficial reading of the King James text might conceivably lead to that conclusion, but the truth is that Christ taught not the coming of the Holy Spirit *and* power, but the coming of the Holy Spirit *as* power; the power and the Spirit are the same.

Our mother tongue is a beautiful and facile instrument, but it can also be a tricky and misleading one, and for this reason it must be used with care if we would avoid giving and receiving wrong impressions by its means. Especially is this true when we are speaking of God, for God being wholly unlike anything or anybody in His universe our very thoughts of Him as well as our words are in constant danger of going astray. One example is found in the words, "The power of God." The danger is that we think of "power" as something belonging to God as muscular energy belongs to a man, as something which He *has* and which might be separated from Him and still have existence in itself. We must remember that the "attributes" of

56

God are not component parts of the blessed Godhead nor elements out of which He is composed. A god who could be *composed* would not be God at all but the work of something or someone greater than he, great enough to compose him. We would then have a synthetic God made out of the pieces we call attributes, and the true God would be another Being altogether, One indeed who is above all thought and all conceiving.

The Bible and Christian theology teach that God is an indivisible Unity, being what He is in undivided oneness, from Whom nothing can be taken and to Whom nothing can be added. Mercy, for instance, immutability, eternity, these are but names which we have given to something which God has declared to be true of Himself. All the "of God" expressions in the Bible must be understood to mean not what God has but *what God is* in His undivided and indivisible Unity. Even the word "nature" when applied to God should be understood as an accommodation to our human way of looking at things and not as an accurate description of anything true of the mysterious Godhead. God has said, "I am that I am," and we can only repeat in reverence, "O God, Thou art."

Our Lord before His ascension said to His disciples, "Tarry in the city of Jerusalem until ye be endued with power from on high." That word *until* is a time-word; it indicates a point in relation to which everything is either before or after. So the experience of those disciples could be stated like this: Up to that point they *had not* received the power; at that point they *did* receive the power; after that point they *had* received the power. Such is the plain historic fact. Power came upon the Church, such power as had never been released into human nature before (with the lone exception of that mighty anointing which came upon Christ at the waters of Jordan). That power, still active in the Church, has enabled her to exist for nearly twenty centuries, even though for all of that time she has remained a highly unpopular minority group among the nations of mankind and has always been surrounded by enemies who would gladly have ended her existence if they could have done so.

"Ye shall receive power." By those words our Lord raised the expectation of His disciples and taught them to look forward to the coming of a supernatural potency into their natures from a source outside of themselves. It was to be something previously unknown to them, but suddenly to come upon them from another world. It was to be nothing less than God himself entering into them with the purpose of ultimately reproducing His own likeness within them.

Here is the dividing line that separates Christianity from all occultism and from every kind of oriental cult ancient or modern. These are all built around the same ideas, varying only in minor details, each with its own peculiar set of phrases and apparently vying with each other in vagueness and obscurity. They each advise, "Get in tune with the Infinite," or "Wake the giant within you," or "Tune in to your hidden potentialities," or "Learn to think creatively." All this may have some fleeting value as a psychological shot in the arm, but its results are not permanent because at its best it builds its hopes upon the fallen nature of man and knows no invasion from above. And whatever may be said in its favor, *it most certainly is not Christianity*.

Christianity takes for granted the absence of any self-help and offers a power which is nothing less than the power of God. This power is to come upon powerless men as a gentle but resistless invasion from another world bringing a moral potency infinitely beyond anything that might be stirred up from within. This power is sufficient; no additional help is needed, no auxiliary source of spiritual energy, for it is the Holy Spirit of God come where the weakness lay to supply power and grace to meet the moral need.

Set over against such a mighty provision as this ethical

Christianity (if I may be allowed the term) is seen to be no Christianity at all. An infantile copying of Christ's "ideals," a pitiable effort to carry out the teachings of the Sermon on the Mount! All this is but religious child's play and is not the faith of Christ and the New Testament.

"Ye shall receive power." This was and is a unique afflatus, an enduement of supernatural energy affecting every department of the believer's life and remaining with him forever. It is not physical power nor even mental power though it may touch everything both mental and physical in its benign outworkings. It is too another kind of power than that seen in nature, in the lunar attraction that creates the tides or the angry flash that splits the great oak during a storm. This power from God operates on another level and affects another department of His wide creation. It is spiritual power. It is the kind of power that God is. It is the ability to achieve spiritual and moral ends. Its long range result is to produce God-like character in men and women who were once wholly evil by nature and by choice.

Now how does this power operate? At its purest it is an unmediated force directly applied by the Spirit of God to the spirit of man. The wrestler achieves his ends by the pressure of his physical body upon the body of his opponent, the teacher by the pressure of ideas upon the mind of the student, the moralist by the pressure of duty upon the conscience of the disciple. So the Holy Spirit performs His blessed work by direct contact with the human spirit.

It would be less than accurate to say that the power of God is always experienced in a direct and unmediated form, for when He so wills the Spirit may use other means as Christ used spittle to heal a blind man. But always the power is above and beyond the means. While the Spirit may use appropriate means to bless a believing man, He never need do so for they are at best but temporary concessions made to our ignorance and unbelief. Where adequate power is present almost any means will suffice, but where

the power is absent not all the means in the world can
secure the desired end. The Spirit of God may use a song,
a sermon, a good deed, a text or the mystery and majesty
of nature, but always the final work will be done by the
pressure of the inliving Spirit upon the human heart.

In the light of this it will be seen how empty and meaningless is the average church service today. All the means
are in evidence; the one ominous weakness is the absence
of the Spirit's power. The form of godliness is there, and
often the form is perfected till it is an aesthetic triumph.
Music and poetry, art and oratory, symbolic vesture and
solemn tones combine to charm the mind of the worship-
per, but too often the supernatural afflatus is not there.
The power from on high is neither known nor desired by
pastor or people. This is nothing less than tragic, and all
the more so because it falls within the field of religion
where the eternal destinies of men are involved.

To the absence of the Spirit may be traced that vague
sense of unreality which almost everywhere invests religion in our times. In the average church service the most
real thing is the shadowy unreality of everything. The wor-
shipper sits in a state of suspended mentation; a kind of
dreamy numbness creeps upon him; he hears words but
they do not register, he cannot relate them to anything on
his own life-level. He is conscious of having entered a kind
of half-world; his mind surrenders itself to a more or less
pleasant mood which passes with the benediction leaving
no trace behind. It does not affect anything in his everyday
life. He is aware of no power, no Presence, no spiritual
reality. There is simply nothing in his experience corre-
sponding to the things which he heard from the pulpit or
sang in the hymns.

One meaning of the word "power" is "ability to do."
There precisely is the wonder of the Spirit's work in the
Church and in the hearts of Christians, His sure ability to
make spiritual things real to the soul. This power can go
straight to its object with piercing directness; it can diffuse

itself through the mind like an infinitely fine volatile essence securing ends above and beyond the limits of the intellect. Reality is its subject matter, reality in heaven and upon earth. It does not create objects which are not there but reveals objects already present and hidden from the soul. In actual human experience this is likely to be the first felt in a heightened sense of the Presence of Christ. He is felt to be a real Person and to be intimately, ravishingly near. Then all other spiritual objects begin to stand out clearly before the mind. Grace, forgiveness, cleansing take on a form of almost bodily clearness. Prayer loses its unmeaning quality and becomes a sweet conversation with Someone actually there. Love for God and for the children of God takes possession of the soul. We feel ourselves near to heaven and it is now the earth and the world that begin to seem unreal. We know them now for what they are, realities indeed, but like stage scenery here for one brief hour and soon to pass away. The world to come takes on a hard outline before our minds and begins to invite our interest and our devotion. Then the whole life changes to suit the new reality and the change is permanent. Slight fluctuations there may be like the rise and dip of the line on a graph, but the established direction is upward and the ground taken is held.

This is not all, but it will give a fair idea of what is meant when the New Testament speaks of *power*, and perhaps by contrast we may learn how little of the power we enjoy.

I think there can be no doubt that the need above all other needs in the Church of God at this moment is the power of the Holy Spirit. More education, better organization, finer equipment, more advanced methods—all are unavailing. It is like bringing a better pulmotor after the patient is dead. Good as these things are they can never give life. "It is the Spirit that quickeneth." Good as they are they can never bring power. "Power belongeth unto God." Protestantism is on the wrong road when it tries to win merely by means of a "united front." It is not organizational unity we need most; the great need is power. The headstones in the cemetery present a united front, but they stand mute and helpless while the world passes by.

I suppose my suggestion will not receive much serious attention, but I should like to suggest that we Bible-believing Christians announce a moratorium on religious activity and set our house in order preparatory to the coming of an afflatus from above. So carnal is the body of Christians which composes the conservative wing of the Church, so shockingly irreverent are our public services in some quarters, so degraded are our religious tastes in still others, that the need for power could scarcely have been greater at any time in history. I believe we should profit immensely were we to declare a period of silence and self-examination during which each one of us searched his own heart and sought to meet every condition for a real baptism of power from on high.

We may be sure of one thing, that for our deep trouble there is no cure apart from a visitation, yes, an *invasion* of power from above. Only the Spirit Himself can show us what is wrong with us and only the Spirit can prescribe the cure. Only the Spirit can save us from the numbing unreality of Spiritless Christianity. Only the Spirit can show us the Father and the Son. Only the inworking of the Spirit's power can discover to us the solemn majesty and the heart ravishing mystery of the Triune God.

8

The Holy Spirit as Fire

*And there appeared unto them
cloven tongues like as of fire,
And it sat upon each of them.*

Acts 2:3

Christian theology teaches that God in His essential nature is both inscrutable and ineffable. This by simple definition means that He is incapable of being searched into or understood, and that He cannot tell forth or utter what He is. This inability lies not in God but in the limitations of our creaturehood. "Why inquirest thou after my name, for it is secret?" Only God knows God in any final meaning of the word *know*. "Even so the things of God knoweth no man, but the Spirit of God."

To the average Christian today this may sound strange, if not downright confusing, for the temper of religious thinking in our times is definitely not theological. We may live out a full lifetime and die without once having our minds challenged by the sweet mystery of the Godhead if we depend upon the churches to do the challenging. They are altogether too busy playing with shadows and getting "adjusted" to one thing and another to spend much time thinking about God. It might be well, therefore, to consider for a moment longer the divine inscrutability.

God in His essential Being is unique in the only sense

that word will bear. That is, there is nothing like Him in the universe. What He is cannot be conceived by the mind because He is "altogether other" than anything with which we have had experience before. The mind has no material with which to start. No man has ever entertained a thought which can be said to describe God in any but the vaguest and most imperfect sense. Where God is known at all it must be otherwise than by our creature-reason.

Novatian, in a famous treatise on the Trinity written sometime about the middle of the third century, says, "In all our meditations upon the qualities of the attributes and content of God, we pass beyond our powers of fit conception, nor can human eloquence put forth a power commensurate with His greatness. At the contemplation and utterance of His majesty, all eloquence is rightly dumb, all mental effort is feeble. For God is greater than mind itself. His greatness cannot be conceived. Nay, if we could conceive of His greatness, He would be less than the human mind which could form the conception. He is greater than all language, and no statement can express Him. Indeed, if any statement could express Him, He would be less than human speech, which could by such statement comprehend and gather up all that He is. Up to a certain point, of course, we can have experience of Him, without language, but no man can express in words all that He is in Himself. Suppose, for instance, one speaks of Him as light; this is an account of part of His creation, not of Himself. It does not express what He is. Or suppose one speaks of Him as power. This too sets forth in words His attribute of might, rather than His being. Or suppose one speaks of Him as majesty. Once again, we have a declaration of the honor which is His Own, rather than of Him in Himself. . . . To sum up the matter in a single sentence, every possible statement that can be made about God expresses some possession or virtue of God, rather than God Himself. What words or thoughts are worthy of Him, Who is above all language and all thought? The conception of God as He is can only be grasped in one way, and even that is impossible for us, beyond our grasp and understanding; by thinking of Him as a Being Whose attributes and greatness are·beyond our powers of understanding, or even of thought."

Just because God cannot tell us *what He is* He very often tells us *what He is like.* By these "like" figures He leads our faltering minds as close as they can come to that "Light which no man can approach unto." Through the more cumbersome medium of the intellect the soul is prepared for the moment when it can, through the operation of the Holy Spirit, know God as He is in Himself. God has used a number of these similitudes to hint at His incomprehensible being, and judging from the Scriptures one would gather that *His favorite similitude is fire.* In one place the Spirit speaks expressly, "For our God is a consuming fire." This accords with His revelation of Himself as recorded throughout the Bible. As a fire He spoke to Moses from the burning bush; in the fire He dwelt above the camp of Israel through all the wilderness journey; as fire He dwelt between the wings of the cherubim in the Holy of Holies; to Ezekiel He revealed Himself as a strange brightness of "a fire infolding itself." "I saw as it were the appearance of a fire and it had a brightness round about. As the appearance of the bow that is in the cloud in the day of rain, so was the appearance of the brightness round about. This was the appearance of the likeness of the glory of the Lord. And when I saw it, I fell on my face, and I heard a voice of one that spake" (Ezek. 1:27-28).

With the coming of the Holy Spirit at Pentecost the same imagery was continued. "And there appeared unto them cloven tongues like as of fire, and it sat upon each of them." That which came upon the disciples in that upper room was nothing less than God Himself. To their mortal eyes He appeared as fire, and may we not safely conclude that those Scripture-taught believers knew at once what it meant? The God who had appeared to them as fire throughout all their long history was now dwelling in them as fire. He had moved from without to the interior of their lives. The Shekinah that had once blazed over the mercy seat now blazed on their foreheads as an external emblem of the fire that had invaded their natures. This was Deity giving Himself to ransomed men. The flame was the seal of a new union. They were now men and women of the Fire.

Here is the whole final message of the New Testament: Through the atonement in Jesus' blood sinful men may now become one with God. Deity indwelling men! That is Christianity in its fullest effectuation, and even those greater glories of the world to come will be in essence but a greater and more perfect experience of the soul's union with God.

Deity indwelling men! That, I say, is Christianity, and no man has experienced rightly the power of Christian belief until he has known this for himself as a living reality. Everything else is preliminary to this. Incarnation, atonement, justification, regeneration; what are these but acts of God preparatory to the work of invading and the act of indwelling the redeemed human soul? Man who moved out of the heart of God by sin now moves back into the heart of God by redemption. God who moved out of the heart of man because of sin now enters again His ancient dwelling to drive out His enemies and once more make the place of His feet glorious.

That visible fire on the day of Pentecost had for the Church a deep and tender significance, for it told to all ages that they upon whose heads it sat were men and women apart; they were "creatures out of the fire" as surely as were they whom Ezekiel in his vision saw by the river Chebar. The mark of the fire was the sign of divinity; they who received it were forever a peculiar people, sons and daughters of the Flame.

One of the most telling blows which the enemy ever struck at the life of the Church was to create in her a fear of the Holy Spirit. No one who mingles with Christians in these times will deny that such a fear exists. Few there are who without restraint will open their whole heart to the blessed Comforter. He has been and is so widely misunderstood that the very mention of His Name in some circles is enough to frighten many people into resistance. The source of this unreasoning fear may easily be traced, but it would be a fruitless labor to do it here. Sufficient to say that the fear is groundless. Perhaps we may help to destroy its power over us if we examine that fire which is the symbol of the Spirit's Person and Presence.

The Holy Spirit is first of all *a moral flame*. It is not an accident of language that He is called the *Holy* Spirit, for whatever else the word *holy* may mean it does undoubtedly carry with it the idea of moral purity. And the Spirit, being God, must be absolutely and infinitely pure. With Him there are not (as with men) grades and degrees of holiness. He is holiness itself, the sum and essence of all that is unspeakably pure.

No one whose senses have been exercised to know good and evil but must grieve over the sight of zealous souls seeking to be filled with the Holy Spirit while they are yet living in a state of moral carelessness or borderline sin. Such a thing is a moral contradiction. Whoever would be filled and indwelt by the Spirit should first judge his life for any hidden iniquities; he should courageously expel from his heart everything which is out of accord with the character of God as revealed by the Holy Scriptures.

At the base of all true Christian experience must lie a sound and sane morality. No joys are valid, no delights legitimate where sin is allowed to live in life or conduct. No transgression of pure righteousness dare excuse itself on the ground of superior religious experience. To seek high emotional states while living in sin is to throw our whole life open to self deception and the judgment of God. "Be ye holy" is not a mere motto to be framed and hung on the wall. It is a serious commandment from the Lord of the whole earth. "Cleanse your hands, ye sinners; and purify your hearts, ye double minded. Be afflicted, and mourn, and weep: let your laughter be turned into mourning, and your joy into heaviness" (James 4:8–9). The true Christian ideal is not to be happy but to be holy. The holy heart alone can be the habitation of the Holy Ghost.

The Holy Spirit is also a *spiritual flame.* He alone can raise our worship to true spiritual levels. For we might as well know once for all that morality and ethics, however lofty, are still not Christianity. The faith of Christ undertakes to raise the soul to actual communion with God, to introduce into our religious experiences a supra-rational element as far above mere goodness as the heavens are above the earth. The coming of the Spirit brought to the Book of Acts this very quality of supramundaneness, this mysterious elevation of tone not found in as high intensity even in the Gospels. The key of the Book of Acts is definitely the major. There is in it no trace of creature-sadness, no lingering disappointment, no quaver of uncertainty. The mood is heavenly. A victorious spirit is found there, a spirit which could never be the result of mere religious belief. The joy of the first Christians was not the joy of logic working on facts. They did not reason, "Christ is risen from the dead; therefore we ought to be glad." Their gladness was as great a miracle as the resurrection itself; indeed these were and are organically related. The moral happiness of the Creator had taken residence in the breasts of redeemed creatures and they could not but be glad.

The flame of the Spirit is also *intellectual.* Reason, say the theologians, is one of the divine attributes. There need be no incompatibility between the deepest experiences of the Spirit and the highest attainments of the human intellect. *It is only required that the Christian intellect be fully surrendered to God and there need be no limit to its activities* beyond those imposed upon it by its own strength and size. How cold and deadly is the unblessed intellect. A superior brain without the saving essence of godliness may turn against the human race and drench the world with blood, or worse, it may loose ideas into the earth which will continue to curse mankind for centuries after it has turned to dust again. But a Spirit-filled mind is a joy to God and a delight to all men of good will. What would the world have missed if it had been deprived of the love-filled mind of a David or a John or an Isaac Watts?

We naturally shy away from superlatives and from comparisons which praise one virtue at the expense of another, yet I wonder whether there is on earth anything as exquisitely lovely as a brilliant mind aglow with the love of God. Such a mind sheds a mild and healing ray which can actually be *felt* by those who come near it. Virtue goes forth from it and blesses those who merely touch the hem of its garment. One has, for instance, but to read *The Celestial Country,* by Bernard of Cluny, to understand what I mean. There a sensitive and shining intellect warm with the fire of the inliving Spirit writes with a vast and tender sympathy of those longings for immortality which have dwelt deep in the human breast since the first man kneeled down upon the earth out of whose bosom he came and into whose bosom he must soon return again. For loftiness of concept, for sheer triumph of the Christian spirit over mortality, for ability to rest the soul and raise the mind to rapturous worship its equal is hardly found anywhere in uninspired literature. I submit it as my respectful opinion that this single hymn may have ministered more healing virtue to distressed spirits than all the writings of secular poets and philosophers since the art of writing was invented. No unblessed intellect, however sure its genius, would be remotely capable of producing such a work. One closes the book after reading it with the feeling, yes the solemn conviction, that he has heard the voice of the cherubim and the sound of harpers strumming beside the sea of God.

This same feeling of near-inspiration is experienced also in the letters of Samuel Rutherford, in the *Te Deum,* in many of the hymns of Watts and Wesley, and occasionally in a work of some lesser known saint whose limited gifts may have been for one joyous moment made incandescent by the fire of the indwelling Spirit.

The blight of the Pharisee's heart in olden times was doctrine without love. With the teachings of the Pharisees Christ had little quarrel, but with the pharisaic spirit He carried on unceasing warfare to the end. It was religion that put Christ on the cross, religion without the indwelling Spirit. It is no use to deny that Christ was crucified by persons who would today be called Fundamentalists. This should prove most disquieting if not downright distressing to us who pride ourselves on our orthodoxy. An unblessed soul filled with the letter of truth may actually be worse off than a pagan kneeling before a fetish. We are safe only when the love of God is shed abroad in our hearts by the Holy Ghost, only when our intellects are indwelt by the loving Fire that came at Pentecost. For the Holy Spirit is not a luxury, not something added now and again to produce a de luxe type of Christian once in a generation. No, He is for every child of God a vital necessity, and that He fill and indwell His people is more than a languid hope. It is rather an inescapable imperative.

The Spirit is also a *volitional flame.* Here as elsewhere the imagery is inadequate to express all the truth, and unless care is taken we may easily gain a wrong impression from its use. For fire as we see and know it every day is a *thing*, not a person, and for that reason it has no will of its own. But the Holy Spirit is a Person, having those attributes of personality of which volition is one. He does not, upon entering the human soul, void any of His attributes, nor does He surrender them in part or in full to the soul into which He enters. Remember, the Holy Spirit is Lord. "Now the Lord is that Spirit," said Paul to the Corinthians. The Nicene Creed says, "And I believe in the Holy Ghost, the Lord and Giver of Life," and the Athanasian Creed declares, "So likewise the Father is Lord, the Son Lord, and the Holy Ghost Lord. And yet not three Lords: but one Lord." Whatever problems this may pose for the understanding, our faith must accept it and make it a part of our total belief about God and the Spirit. Now it hardly need be said that the Sovereign Lord will never abandon the prerogatives of His Godhood. Wherever He is He must continue to act like Himself. When He enters the human heart He will be there what He has always been, Lord in His own right.

The deep disease of the human heart is a will broken loose from its center, like a planet which has left its central sun and started to revolve around some strange body from outer space which may have moved in close enough to draw it away. When Satan said, "I will," he broke loose from his normal center, and the disease with which he has infected the human race is the disease of disobedience and revolt. Any adequate scheme of redemption must take into account this revolt and must undertake to restore again the human will to its proper place in the will of God. In accord with this underlying need for the healing of the will, the Holy Spirit, when He effects His gracious invasion of the believing heart, must win that heart to glad and voluntary obedience to the whole will of God. The cure must be wrought from within; no outward conformity will do. Until the will is sanctified the man is still a rebel just as an outlaw is still an outlaw at heart even though he may be yielding grudging obedience to the sheriff who is taking him to prison.

The Holy Spirit achieves this inward cure by merging the will of the redeemed man with His own. This is not accomplished at one stroke. There must be, it is true, some kind of over-all surrender of the will to Christ before any work of grace can be done, but the full mergence of every part of the life with the life of God in the Spirit is likely to be a longer process than we in our creature impatience would wish. The most advanced soul may be shocked and chagrined to discover some private area within his life where he had been, unknown to himself, acting as lord and proprietor of that which he thought he had given to

God. It is the work of the in-living Spirit to point out these moral discrepancies and correct them. He does not, as is sometimes said, "break" the human will, but He does invade it and bring it gently to a joyous union with the will of God.

To will the will of God is to do more than give unprotesting consent to it; it is rather to choose God's will with positive determination. As the work of God advances the Christian finds himself free to choose whatever he will, and he gladly chooses the will of God as his highest conceivable good. Such a man has found life's highest goal. He has been placed beyond the little disappointments that plague the rest of men. Whatever happens to him is the will of God for him and that is just what he most ardently desires. But it is only fair to state that this condition is one not reached by many of the busy Christians of our busy times. Until it is reached, however, the Christian's peace cannot be complete. There must be still a certain inward controversy, a sense of spiritual disquiet which poisons our joy and greatly reduces our power.

Another quality of the in-dwelling Fire is *emotion*. This must be understood in the light of what has been said before about the divine inscrutability. What God is in His unique essence cannot be discovered by the mind nor uttered by the lips, but those qualities in God which may be termed rational, and so received by the intellect, have been freely set forth in the sacred Scriptures. They do not tell us what God is, but they do tell us what God is like, and the sum of them constitute a mental picture of the Divine Being seen as it were afar off and through a glass darkly.

Now the Bible teaches that there is something in God which is like emotion. He experiences something which is like our love, something that is like our grief, that is like our joy. And we need not fear to go along with this conception of what God is like. Faith would easily draw the inference that since we were made in His image He would have qualities like our own. But such an inference, while satisfying to the mind, is not the ground of our belief. *God has said certain things about Himself, and these furnish all the grounds we require.* "The Lord thy God in the midst of thee is mighty; he will save, he will rejoice over thee with joy; he will rest in his love, he will joy over thee with singing" (Zeph. 3:17). This is but one verse among thousands which serve to form our rational picture of what God is like, and they tell us plainly that God feels something like our love, like our joy, and what He feels makes Him act very much as we would in a similar situation; He rejoices over His loved ones with joy and singing.

Here is emotion on as high a plane as it can ever be seen, emotion flowing out of the heart of God Himself. Feeling, then, is not the degenerate son of unbelief that it is often painted by some of our Bible teachers. Our ability to feel is one of the marks of our divine origin. We need not be ashamed of either tears or laughter. The Christian stoic who has crushed his feelings is only two-thirds of a man; an important third part has been repudiated.

Holy feeling had an important place in the life of our Lord. "For the joy that was set before Him" He endured the cross and despised its shame. He pictured Himself crying, "Rejoice with me, for I have found my sheep which was lost." On the night of His agony He "sang an hymn" before going out to the Mount of Olives. After His resurrection He sang among His brethren in the great congregation (Ps. 22:22). And if the Song of Solomon refers to Christ (as most Christians believe it does) then how are we to miss the sound of His rejoicing as He brings His bride home after the night has ended and the shadows have fled away?

One of the very greatest calamities which sin has brought upon us is the debasement of our normal emotions. We laugh at things which are not funny; we find pleasure in acts which are beneath our human dignity; and we rejoice in objects which should have no place in our affections. The objection to "sinful pleasures" which has always been characteristic of the true saint, is at bottom simply a protest against the degradation of our human emotions. That gambling, for instance, should be allowed to engross the interests of men made in the image of God has seemed like a horrible perversion of noble powers; that alcohol should be necessary to stimulate the feeling of pleasure has seemed like a kind of prostitution; that men should turn to the man-made theatre for enjoyment has seemed an affront to the God who placed us in the midst of a universe charged with high dramatic action. The world's artificial pleasures are all but evidence that the human race has to a large extent lost its power to enjoy the true pleasures of life and is forced to substitute for them false and degrading thrills.

The work of the Holy Spirit is, among other things, to rescue the redeemed man's emotions, to restring his harp and open again the wells of sacred joy which have been stopped up by sin. That He does this is the unanimous testimony of the saints. And it is not inconsistent with the whole way of God in His creation. Pure pleasure is a part of life, such an important part that it is difficult to see how human life could be justified if it were to consist of endless existence devoid of pleasurable feeling.

The Holy Spirit would set an aeolian harp in the window of our souls so that the winds of heaven may play sweet melody for a musical accompaniment to the humblest task we may be called to perform. The spiritual love of Christ will make constant music within our hearts and enable us to rejoice even in our sorrows.

9

The Spirit-Filled Life

. . . be filled with the Spirit.
Eph. 5:18

That every Christian can be and should be filled with the Holy Spirit would hardly seem to be a matter for debate among Christians. Yet some will argue that the Holy Spirit is not for plain Christians but for ministers and missionaries only. Others hold that the measure of the Spirit received at regeneration is identical with that received by the disciples at Pentecost and any hope of additional fullness after conversion simply rests upon error. A few will express a languid hope that some day they may be filled, and still others will avoid the subject as one about which they know very little and which can only cause embarrassment.

I want here boldly to assert that it is my happy belief that every Christian can have a copious outpouring of the Holy Spirit in a measure far beyond that received at conversion, and I might also say, far beyond that enjoyed by the rank and file of orthodox believers today. It is important that we get this straight, for until doubts are removed faith is impossible. God will not surprise a doubting heart with an effusion of the Holy Spirit, nor will He fill anyone who has doctrinal questions about the possibility of being filled.

To remove doubts and create a confident expectation I

recommend a reverent study of the Word of God itself. I am willing to rest my case upon the teachings of the New Testament. If a careful and humble examination of the words of Christ and His apostles does not lead to a belief that we may be filled with the Holy Spirit now, then I see no reason to look elsewhere. For it matters little what this or that religious teacher has said for or against the proposition. If the doctrine is not taught in the Scriptures then it cannot be supported by any argument, and all exhortations to be filled are valueless.

I shall not here present a case for the affirmative. Let the inquirer examine the evidence for himself, and if he decides that there is no warrant in the New Testament for believing that he can be filled with the Spirit, let him shut this book and save himself the trouble of reading further. What I say from here on is addressed to men and women who have gotten over their questions and are confident that when they meet the conditions they may indeed be filled with the Holy Spirit.

Before a man can be filled with the Spirit *he must be sure he wants to be.* And let this be taken seriously. Many Christians want to be filled, but their desire is a vague romantic kind of thing hardly worthy to be called desire. They have almost no knowledge of what it will cost them to realize it.

Let us imagine that we are talking to an inquirer, some eager young Christian, let us say, who has sought us out to learn about the Spirit-filled life. As gently as possible, considering the pointed nature of the questions, we would probe his soul somewhat as follows: "Are you sure you want to be filled with a Spirit who, though He is like Jesus in His gentleness and love, will nevertheless demand to be Lord of your life? Are you willing to let your personality be taken over by another, even if that other be the Spirit of God Himself? If the Spirit takes charge of your life He will expect unquestioning obedience in everything. He will not tolerate in you the self-sins even though they are permitted and excused by most Christians. By the self-sins I mean self-love, self-pity, self-seeking, self-confidence, self-righteousness, self-aggrandizement, self-defense. You will find the Spirit to be in sharp opposition to the easy ways of the world and of the mixed multitude within the precincts of religion. He will be jealous over you for good. He will not allow you to boast or swagger or show off. He will take the direction of your life away from you. He will reserve the right to test you, to discipline you, to chasten you for your soul's sake. He may strip you of many of those borderline pleasures which other Christians enjoy but which are to you a source of refined evil. Through it all He will enfold you in a love so vast, so mighty, so all-embracing, so wondrous that your very losses will seem like gains and your small pains like pleasures. Yet the flesh will whimper under His yoke and cry out against it as a burden too great to bear. And you will be permitted to enjoy the solemn privilege of suffering to 'fill up that which is behind of the afflictions of Christ' in your flesh for His body's sake, which is the Church. Now, with the conditions before you, do you still want to be filled with the Holy Spirit?"

If this appears severe, let us remember that the way of the cross is never easy. The shine and glamour accompanying popular religious movements is as false as the sheen on the wings of the angel of darkness when he for a moment transforms himself into an angel of light. The spiritual timidity that fears to show the cross in its true character is not on any grounds to be excused. It can result only in disappointment and tragedy at last.

Before we can be filled with the Spirit *the desire to be filled must be all-consuming*. It must be for the time the biggest thing in the life, so acute, so intrusive as to crowd out everything else. The degree of fullness in any life accords perfectly with the intensity of true desire. We have as much of God as we actually want. One great hindrance to the Spirit-filled life is the theology of complacency so widely accepted among gospel Christians today. According to this view acute desire is an evidence of unbelief and proof of lack of knowledge of the Scriptures. A sufficient refutation of this position is afforded by the Word of God itself and by the fact that it always fails to produce real saintliness among those who hold it.

Then, I doubt whether anyone ever received that divine afflatus with which we are here concerned who did not first *experience a period of deep anxiety and inward agitation*. Religious contentment is the enemy of the spiritual life always. The biographies of the saints teach that the way to spiritual greatness has always been through much suffering and inward pain. The phrase, "the way of the cross," though it has come in certain circles to denote something very beautiful, even enjoyable, still means to the real Christian what it has always meant, the way of rejection and loss. No one ever enjoyed a cross, just as no one ever enjoyed a gallows.

The Christian who is seeking better things and who has to his consternation found himself in a state of complete self-despair need not be discouraged. Despair with self, where it is accompanied by faith, is a good friend, for it destroys one of the heart's most potent enemies and prepares the soul for the ministration of the Comforter. A sense of utter emptiness, of disappointment and darkness can (if we are alert and wise to what is going on) be the shadow in the valley of shadows that leads on to those fruitful fields that lie further in. If we misunderstand it and resist this visitation of God we may miss entirely every benefit a kind heavenly Father has in mind for us. If we cooperate with God He will take away the natural comforts which have served us as mother and nurse for so long and put us where we can receive no help except from the Comforter Himself. He will tear away that false thing the Chinese call "face" and show us how painfully small we really are. When He is finished with us we will know what our Lord meant when He said, "Blessed are the poor in spirit."

Be sure, however, that in these painful chastenings we shall not be deserted by our God. He will never leave us nor forsake us, nor will He be wroth with us nor rebuke us. He will not break His covenant nor alter that which has gone out of His mouth. He will keep us as the apple of His eye and watch over us as a mother watches over her child. His love will not fail even while He is taking us through this experience of self-crucifixion so real, so terrible, that we can express it only by crying, "My God, my God, why hast Thou forsaken me?"

Now let us keep our theology straight about all this. There is not in this painful stripping one remote thought of human merit. The "dark night of the soul" knows not one dim ray of the treacherous light of self-righteousness. We do not by suffering earn the anointing for which we yearn, nor does this devastation of soul make us dear to God nor give us additional favor in His eyes. The value of the stripping experience lies in its power to detach us from life's passing interests and to throw us back upon eternity. It serves to empty our earthly vessels and prepare us for the inpouring of the Holy Spirit.

The filling with the Spirit, then, requires that we give up our all, that we undergo an inward death, that we rid our hearts of that centuries-old accumulation of Adamic trash and open all rooms to the heavenly Guest.

The Holy Spirit is a living Person and should be treated as a person. We must never think of Him as a blind energy nor as an impersonal force. He hears and sees and feels as any person does. He speaks and hears us speak. We can please Him or grieve Him or silence Him as we can any other person. He will respond to our timid effort to know Him and will ever meet us over half the way.

However wonderful the crisis-experience of being filled with the Spirit, we should remember that it is only a means toward something greater: that greater thing is the life-long walk in the Spirit, indwelt, directed, taught and empowered by His mighty Person. And to continue thus to walk in the Spirit requires that we meet certain conditions. These are laid down for us in the sacred Scriptures and are there for all to see.

The Spirit-filled walk demands, for instance, that we live in the Word of God as a fish lives in the sea. By this I do not mean that we study the Bible merely, nor that we take a "course" in Bible doctrine. I mean that we should "mediate day and night" in the sacred Word, that we should love it and feast upon it and digest it every hour of the day and night. When the business of life compels our attention we may yet, by a kind of blessed mental reflex, keep the Word of Truth ever before our minds.

Then if we would please the in-dwelling Spirit we must be all taken up with Christ. The Spirit's present work is to honor Him, and everything He does has this for its ultimate purpose. And we must make our thoughts a clean sanctuary for His holy habitation. He dwells in our thoughts, and soiled thoughts are as repugnant to Him as soiled linen to a king. Above all we must have a cheerful faith that will keep on believing however radical the fluctuation in our emotional states may be.

The Spirit in-dwelt life is not a special de luxe edition of Christianity to be enjoyed by a certain rare and privileged few who happen to be made of finer and more sensitive stuff than the rest. Rather, it is the normal state for every redeemed man and woman the world over. It is "that mystery which hath been hid from ages and from generations, but now is made manifest to his saints: to whom God would make known what is the riches of the glory of this mystery among the gentiles: which is Christ in you, the hope of glory" (Col. 1:26). Faber, in one of his sweet and reverent hymns, addressed this good word to the Holy Spirit:

> *Ocean, wide flowing Ocean, Thou*
> *Of uncreated Love;*

I tremble as within my soul
I feel Thy waters move.

Thou art a sea without a shore;
Awful, immense Thou art;
A sea which can contract itself
Within my narrow heart.

10

Faith Is a Journey, Not a Destination

And they continued steadfastly in the apostles' doctrine and fellowship, and in breaking of bread, and in prayers.

Acts 2:42

So says Luke of the thousands who received the Word and were baptized following the preaching of Peter on the day of Pentecost.

Conversion for those first Christians was not a destination; it was the beginning of a journey. And right there is where the Biblical emphasis differs from ours.

Today all is made to depend upon the initial act of believing. At a given moment a "decision" is made for Christ, and after that everything is automatic. This is not taught in so many words, but such is the impression inadvertently created by our failure to lay a scriptural emphasis in our evangelistic preaching. We of the evangelical churches are almost all guilty of this lopsided view of the Christian life, and because the foundations are out of plumb the temple of God leans dangerously and threatens to topple unless some immediate corrections are made.

In our eagerness to make converts we allow our hearers to absorb the idea that they can deal with their entire responsibility once and for all by an act of believing. This is in some vague way supposed to honor grace and glorify God, whereas actually it is to make Christ the author of a grotesque, unworkable system that has no counterpart in the Scriptures of truth.

In the Book of Acts faith was for each believer a beginning, not an end; it was a journey, not a bed in which to lie while waiting for the day of our Lord's triumph. Believing was not a once-done act; it was more than an act, it was an attitude of heart and mind which inspired and enabled the believer to take up his cross and follow the Lamb whithersoever He went.

"They continued," says Luke, and is it not plain that it was only by continuing that they could confirm their faith? On a given day they believed, were baptized and joined themselves to the believing company. Very good, but tomorrow what? and the next day? and the next week? How could anyone know that their conversion had been genuine? How could they live down the critic's charge that they had been pressured into a decision? that they had cracked under the psychological squeeze set up by crowds and religious excitement? Obviously there was only one way: They continued.

Not only did they continue, they continued steadfastly. So wrote Luke, and the word "steadfastly" is there to tell us that they continued against serious opposition. Steadfastness is required only when we are under attack, mental or physical, and the story of those early Christians is a story of faith under fire. The opposition was real.

Here again is seen the glaring discrepancy between Biblical Christianity and that of present-day evangelicals, particularly in the United States. In certain countries, I am told, some of our brethren are suffering painful persecution and counting not their lives dear unto themselves that they might win Christ. For these I have only utmost admiration. I speak not of such as they, but of the multitudes of religious weaklings within our evangelical fold here in America.

To make converts here we are forced to play down the difficulties and play up the peace of mind and worldly success enjoyed by those who accept Christ. We must assure our hearers that Christianity is now a proper and respectable thing and that Christ has become quite popular with political bigwigs, well-to-do business tycoons and the Hollywood swimming pool set. Thus assured, hell-deserving sinners are coming in droves to "accept" Christ for what they can get out of Him; and though one now and again may drop a tear as proof of his sincerity, it is hard to escape the conclusion that most of them are stooping to patronize the Lord of glory much as a young couple might fawn on a boresome but rich old uncle in order to be mentioned in his will later on.

We will never be completely honest with our hearers until we tell them the blunt truth that as members of a race of moral rebels they are in a serious jam, and one they will not get out of easily. If they refuse to repent and believe on Christ they will most surely perish; if they do turn to Him, the same enemies that crucified Him will try to crucify them. One way they suffer alone without hope; the other way they suffer with Christ for a while, but in the midst of their suffering they enjoy His loving consolation and inward support and are able to rejoice even in tribulation.

Those first believers turned to Christ with the full understanding that they were espousing an unpopular cause that could cost them everything. They knew they would henceforth be members of a hated minority group with life and liberty always in jeopardy.

This is no idle flourish. Shortly after Pentecost some were jailed, many lost all their earthly goods, a few were slain outright and hundreds "scattered abroad."

They could have escaped all this by the simple expedient of denying their faith and turning back to the world; but this they steadfastly refused to do.

Seen thus in comparison with each other, is the Christianity of American evangelicalism today the same as that of the first century? I wonder. But again, I think I know.

11

The Key to Human Life
Is Theological

Anthropology tries to understand man by digging into his past and examining his primitive beginnings. Psychology seeks to understand him by digging into his mind. Philosophy takes whatever data it can assemble about man's external or internal life, past or present, borrows freely from historian and scientist, and reasons from this to the nature of man.

The answer to the question "What is man?" is sought by going straight to men to test and weigh and measure. Skull shape, bone structure, folklore, habits, customs, diet, superstitious practices, religion, social patterns, civil organization, tabus, reactions, emotions and countless other factors are taken into consideration in the search for the answer. The plan is, of course, to determine scientifically what man is by observing on a wide scale and over a long period what he does. But because the technique is wrong the conclusions must be false. It cannot be otherwise.

I well know that I am simply raising here the old question of naturalism versus supernaturalism, a question that has for centuries been fruitlessly debated and left unsettled for each generation to dispose of as it would or could. Were I a philosopher I might properly join the search for the key to life. As a man fully persuaded of the truth of the New Testament evangel and totally committed to Christ, there is for me no question here demanding an answer. That an-

88

swer has been given in the positive and joyous Biblical declaration that God made man in His own image and likeness, akin to the earth as touching his physical body, it is true, but next of kin to heaven in his spirit, which came from God to return to God again (Eccl. 12:7). His body does not hold the key to his true nature; that key is found in his spirit which, while alienated from God by that mighty moral disaster theologians call the Fall, is yet susceptible of reclamation and full restoration to God through the redemption which is in Christ Jesus.

To know man we must begin with God. Secular learning, darkly colored as it is by humanism and rationalism in their various forms, has made a great many present-day Christians afraid to state their true position lest they earn for themselves one or more of the caustic sobriquets by which the wise men of this world stigmatize those who disagree with them; such, for instance, as "transcendentalist," "absolutist" or "supernaturalist."

As for myself, I do not fear such appellations even though they be hurled at me with the purpose of discrediting me once and for all. Far from fearing them, I glory in them. While I do not allow them to retain all the shades of meaning they have gathered to themselves in their journey down the years, I cheerfully accept them as far as they express meanings which I find in the Christian revelation.

No Christian, for instance, need draw back from the word *transcendentalist*, for at the very root of his holy faith is belief in a transcendent world, a world above nature, different from and lying beyond matter and space and time, into which science cannot pry and at whose portals uncomprehending reason can do no other than reverently kneel and adore. Nor should he shrink from the word "supernaturalist," for it quite accurately describes an important tenet in his Christian creed. He does believe that there is a Divinity which shapes our ends. Nature, he holds, cannot account for herself but must humbly point upward to the One who gave her birth and whose invisible presence is her wisdom and her life. This he believes, and he considers everyone who believes less than this to be "finished and finite clods," Esaus who have sold their birthright for a mess of pottage.

Neither does the term *absolutist* make the instructed Christian blush or apologize. However scornfully the word may be spat at him, he is unperturbed. He knows his enemies are angry with him for refusing to accept two of their favorite doctrines, the relativity of morals and the pragmatic nature of religious beliefs. He does not try to deny that he holds with complete dogmatism the scriptural teaching that God is among other things uncreated, self-sufficient, eternal, infinite, sovereign and absolute. He glories in a God absolutely holy, absolutely wise: in short, in a God who is everything that He is absolutely, unaffected by anything external to Himself. Indeed, it is necessary to him that he believe this about God; and if so to believe brands him as an absolutist he is quite happy about the whole thing. He knows what he believes, and words do not frighten him.

The flaw in current evangelism lies in its humanistic approach. It struggles to be supernaturalistic but never quite makes it. It is frankly fascinated by the great, noisy, aggressive world with its big names, its hero worship, its wealth and its garish pageantry. To the millions of disappointed persons who have always yearned for worldly glory but never attained to it, the modern evangel offers a quick and easy short cut to their heart's desire. Peace of mind, happiness, prosperity, social acceptance, publicity, success in sports, business, the entertainment field, and perchance to sit occasionally at the same banquet table with a celebrity—all this on earth and heaven at last. Certainly no insurance company can offer half as much.

In this quasi-Christian scheme of things God becomes the Aladdin lamp who does the bidding of everyone that will accept His Son and sign a card. The total obligation of the sinner is discharged when he accepts Christ. After that he has but to come with his basket and receive the religious equivalent of everything the world offers and enjoy it to the limit. Those who have not accepted Christ must be content with this world, but the Christian gets this one with the one to come thrown in as a bonus.

Such is the Christian message as interpreted by vast numbers of religious leaders today. This gross misapprehension of the truth is back of much (I almost said most) of our present evangelical activity. It determines directions, builds programs, decides the content of sermons, fixes the quality of local churches and even of whole denominations, sets the pattern for religious writers and forms the editorial policy of many evangelical publications.

This concept of Christianity is in radical error, and because it touches the souls of men it is a dangerous, even deadly, error. At bottom it is little more than weak humanism allied with weak Christianity to give it ecclesiastical respectability. It may be identified by its religious approach. Invariably it begins with man and his needs and then looks around for God; true Christianity reveals God as searching for man to deliver him from his ambitions.

Always and always God must be first. The gospel in its scriptural context puts the glory of God first and the salvation of man second. The angels, approaching from above, chanted, "Glory to God in the highest, and on earth peace, good will toward men." This puts the glory of God and the blessing of mankind in their proper order, as do also the opening words of the prayer, "Our Father which art in heaven, hallowed be thy name." Before any petitions are allowed, the name of God must be hallowed. God's glory is and must forever remain the Christian's true point of departure. Anything that begins anywhere else, whatever it is, is certainly not New Testament Christianity.

12

The Tragedy of Wasted Religious Activity

There is probably not another field of human activity where there is so much waste as in the field of religion.

It is altogether possible to waste an hour in church or even in a prayer meeting. The popular "attend the church of your choice" signs that have lately been appearing everywhere may have some small value if they do no more than remind a materialistic civilization that this world is not all and that there are some treasures that cannot be bought with money. Yet we must not forget that a man may attend church for a lifetime and be none the better for it.

In the average church we hear the same prayers repeated each Sunday year in and year out with, one would suspect, not the remotest expectation that they will be answered. It is enough, it seems, that they have been uttered. The familiar phrase, the religious tone, the emotionally loaded words have their superficial and temporary effect, but the worshiper is no nearer to God, no better morally and no surer of heaven than he was before. Yet every Sunday morning for twenty years he goes through the same routine and, allowing two hours for him to leave his house, sit through a church service and return to his house again, he has wasted more than 170 twelve-hour days with this exercise in futility.

The writer to the Hebrews says that some professed

Christians were marking time and getting nowhere. They had had plenty of opportunity to grow, but they had not grown; they had had sufficient time to mature, yet they were still babes; so he exhorted them to leave their meaningless religious round and press on to perfection (Heb. 5:11–6:3).

It is possible to have motion without progress, and this describes much of the activity among Christians today. It is simply lost motion.

In God there is motion, but never wasted motion; He always works toward a predetermined end. Being made in His image, we are by nature constituted so that we are justifying our existence only when we are working with a purpose in mind. Aimless activity is beneath the worth and dignity of a human being. Activity that does not result in progress toward a goal is wasted; yet most Christians have no clear end toward which they are striving. On the endless religious merry-go-round they continue to waste time and energy, of which, God knows, they never had much and have less each hour. This is a tragedy worthy of the mind of an Aeschylus or a Dante.

Back of this tragic waste there is usually one of three causes: The Christian is either ignorant of the Scriptures, unbelieving or disobedient.

I think most Christians are simply uninstructed. They may have been talked into the kingdom when they were only half ready. Any convert made within the last thirty years was almost certainly told that he had but to take Jesus as his personal Saviour and all would be well. Possibly some counselor may have added that he now had eternal life and would most surely go to heaven when he died, if indeed the Lord does not return and carry him away in triumph before the unpleasant moment of death arrives.

After that first hurried entrance into the kingdom there is usually not much more said. The new convert finds himself with a hammer and a saw and no blueprint. He has not the remotest notion what he is supposed to build, so he settles down to the dull routine of polishing his tools once each Sunday and putting them back in their box.

Sometimes, however, the Christian wastes his efforts because of unbelief. Possibly we are all guilty of this to some degree. In our private prayers and in our public services we are forever asking God to do things that He either has already done or cannot do because of our unbelief. We plead for Him to speak when He has already spoken and is at that very moment speaking. We ask Him to come when He is already present and waiting for us to recognize Him. We beg the Holy Spirit to fill us while all the time we are preventing Him by our doubts.

Of course the Christian can hope for no manifestation of God while he lives in a state of disobedience. Let a man refuse to obey God on some clear point, let him set his will stubbornly to resist any commandment of Christ, and the rest of his religious activities will be wasted. He may go to church for fifty years to no profit. He may tithe, teach, preach, sing, write or edit or run a Bible conference till he gets too old to navigate and have nothing but ashes at the last. "To obey is better than sacrifice."

I need only add that all this tragic waste is unnecessary. The believing Christian will relish every moment in church and will profit by it. The instructed, obedient Christian will yield to God as the clay to the potter, and the result will not be waste but glory everlasting.

13

Apprehending God

O taste and see. . . . Ps. 34:8

It was Canon Holmes, of India, who more than twenty-five years ago called attention to the inferential character of the average man's faith in God. To most people God is an inference, not a reality. He is a deduction from evidence which they consider adequate; but He remains personally unknown to the individual. "He *must* be," they say, "therefore we believe He is." Others do not go even so far as this; they know of Him only by hearsay. They have never bothered to think the matter out for themselves, but have heard about Him from others, and have put belief in Him into the back of their minds along with the various odds and ends that make up their total creed. To many others God is but an ideal, another name for goodness, or beauty, or truth; or He is law, or life, or the creative impulse back of the phenomena of existence.

These notions about God are many and varied, but they who hold them have one thing in common: they do not know God in personal experience. The possibility of intimate acquaintance with Him has not entered their minds. While admitting His existence they do not think of Him as knowable in the sense that we know things or people.

Christians, to be sure, go further than this, at least in theory. Their creed requires them to believe in the personality of God, and they have been taught to pray, "Our Father, which art in heaven." Now personality and father-hood carry with them the idea of the possibility of personal acquaintance. This is admitted, I say, in theory, but for millions of Christians, nevertheless, God is no more real than He is to the non-Christian. They go through life try-ing to love an ideal and be loyal to a mere principle.

Over against all this cloudy vagueness stands the clear scriptural doctrine that God can be known in personal ex-perience. A loving Personality dominates the Bible, walk-ing among the trees of the garden and breathing fragrance over every scene. Always a living Person is present, speak-ing, pleading, loving, working, and manifesting Himself whenever and wherever His people have the receptivity necessary to receive the manifestation.

The Bible assumes as a self-evident fact that men can know God with at least the same degree of immediacy as they know any other person or thing that comes within the field of their experience. The same terms are used to ex-press the knowledge of God as are used to express knowl-edge of physical things. "O *taste* and see that the Lord is good." "All thy garments *smell* of myrrh, and aloes, and cassia, out of the ivory palaces." "My sheep *hear* my voice." "Blessed are the pure in heart, for they shall *see* God." These are but four of countless such passages from the Word of God. And more important than any proof text is the fact that the whole import of the Scripture is toward this belief.

What can all this mean except that we have in our hearts organs by means of which we can know God as certainly as we know material things through our familiar five senses? We apprehend the physical world by exercising the facul-ties given us for the purpose, and we possess spiritual faculties by means of which we can know God and the spiritual world if we obey the Spirit's urge and begin to use them.

That a saving work must first be done in the heart is

taken for granted here. The spiritual faculties of the unregenerate man lie asleep in his nature, unused and for every purpose dead; that is the stroke which has fallen upon us by sin. They may be quickened to active life again by the operation of the Holy Spirit in regeneration; that is one of the immeasurable benefits which come to us through Christ's atoning work on the cross.

But the very ransomed children of God themselves: why do they know so little of that habitual conscious communion with God which the Scriptures seem to offer? The answer is our chronic unbelief. Faith enables our spiritual sense to function. Where faith is defective the result will be inward insensibility and numbness toward spiritual things. This is the condition of vast numbers of Christians today. No proof is necessary to support that statement. We have but to converse with the first Christian we meet or enter the first church we find open to acquire all the proof we need.

A spiritual kingdom lies all about us, enclosing us, embracing us, altogether within reach of our inner selves, waiting for us to recognize it. God Himself is here waiting our response to His Presence. This eternal world will come alive to us the moment we begin to reckon upon its reality.

I have just now used two words which demand definition; or if definition is impossible, I must at least make clear what I mean when I use them. They are "reckon" and "reality."

What do I mean by *reality*? I mean that which has existence apart from any idea any mind may have of it, and which would exist if there were no mind anywhere to entertain a thought of it. That which is real has being in itself. It does not depend upon the observer for its validity.

I am aware that there are those who love to poke fun at the plain man's idea of reality. They are the idealists who spin endless proofs that nothing is real outside of the mind. They are the relativists who like to show that there are no fixed points in the universe from which we can measure anything. They smile down upon us from their lofty intellectual peaks and settle us to their own satisfaction by fastening upon us the reproachful term "absolutist." The Christian is not put out of countenance by this show of contempt. He can smile right back at them, for he knows that there is only One who is Absolute, that is God. But he knows also that the Absolute One has made this world for man's uses, and, while there is nothing fixed or real in the last meaning of the words (the meaning as applied to God) *for every purpose of human life we are permitted to act as if there were.* And every man does act thus except the mentally sick. These unfortunates also have trouble with reality, but they are consistent; they insist upon living in accordance with their ideas of things. They are honest, and it is their very honesty that constitutes them a social problem.

The idealists and relativists are not mentally sick. They prove their soundness by living their lives according to the very notions of reality which they in theory repudiate and by counting upon the very fixed points which they prove are not there. They could earn a lot more respect for their notions if they were willing to live by them; but this they are careful not to do. Their ideas are brain-deep, not life-deep. Wherever life touches them they repudiate their theories and live like other men.

The Christian is too sincere to play with ideas for their own sake. He takes no pleasure in the mere spinning of gossamer webs for display. All his beliefs are practical. They are geared into his life. By them he lives or dies, stands or falls for this world and for all time to come. From the insincere man he turns away.

The sincere plain man knows that the world is real. He finds it here when he wakes to consciousness, and he knows that he did not think it into being. It was here waiting for him when he came, and he knows that when he prepares to leave this earthly scene it will be here still to bid him good-bye as he departs. By the deep wisdom of life he is wiser than a thousand men who doubt. He stands upon the earth and feels the wind and rain in his face and he knows that they are real. He sees the sun by day and the stars by night. He sees the hot lightning play out of the dark thundercloud. He hears the sounds of nature and the cries of human joy and pain. These he knows are real. He lies down on the cool earth at night and has no fear that it will prove illusory or fail him while he sleeps. In the morning the firm ground will be under him, the blue sky above him and the rocks and trees around him as when he closed his eyes the night before. So he lives and rejoices in a world of reality.

With his five senses he engages this real world. All things necessary to his physical existence he apprehends by the faculties with which he has been equipped by the God who created him and placed him in such a world as this.

Now, by our definition also God is real. He is real in the absolute and final sense that nothing else is. All other reality is contingent upon His. The great Reality is God who is the Author of that lower and dependent reality which makes up the sum of created things, including ourselves. God has objective existence independent of and apart from any notions which we may have concerning Him. The worshipping heart does not create its Object. It finds Him here when it wakes from its moral slumber in the morning of its regeneration.

Another word that must be cleared up is the word *reckon*. This does not mean to visualize or imagine. Imagination is not faith. The two are not only different from, but stand in sharp opposition to, each other. Imagination projects unreal images out of the mind and seeks to attach reality to them. Faith creates nothing; it simply reckons upon that which is already *there*.

God and the spiritual world are real. We can reckon upon them with as much assurance as we reckon upon the familiar world around us. Spiritual things are there (or rather we should say *here*) inviting our attention and challenging our trust.

Our trouble is that we have established bad thought habits. We habitually think of the visible world as real and doubt the reality of any other. We do not deny the existence of the spiritual world but we doubt that it is real in the accepted meaning of the word.

The world of sense intrudes upon our attention day and night for the whole of our lifetime. It is clamorous, insistent and self-demonstrating. It does not appeal to our faith; it is here, assaulting our five senses, demanding to be accepted as real and final. But sin has so clouded the lenses of our hearts that we cannot see that other reality, the City of God, shining around us. The world of sense triumphs. The visible becomes the enemy of the invisible; the temporal, of the eternal. That is the curse inherited by every member of Adam's tragic race.

At the root of the Christian life lies belief in the invisible. The object of the Christian's faith is unseen reality.

Our uncorrected thinking, influenced by the blindness of our natural hearts and the intrusive ubiquity of visible things, tends to draw a contrast between the spiritual and the real; but actually no such contrast exists. The antithesis lies elsewhere: between the real and the imaginary, between the spiritual and the material, between the temporal and the eternal; but between the spiritual and the real, never. The spiritual *is* real.

If we would rise into that region of light and power plainly beckoning us through the Scriptures of truth we must break the evil habit of ignoring the spiritual. We must shift our interest from the seen to the unseen. For the great unseen Reality is God. "He that cometh to God must believe that he is, and that he is a rewarder of them that diligently seek him." This is basic in the life of faith. From there we can rise to unlimited heights. "Ye believe in God," said our Lord Jesus Christ, "believe also in me." Without the first there can be no second.

If we truly want to follow God we must seek to be other-worldly. This I say knowing well that that word has been used with scorn by the sons of this world and applied to the Christian as a badge of reproach. So be it. Every man must choose his world. If we who follow Christ, with all the facts before us and knowing what we are about, deliberately choose the Kingdom of God as our sphere of interest I see no reason why anyone should object. If we lose by it, the loss is our own; if we gain, we rob no one by so doing. The "other world," which is the object of this world's disdain and the subject of the drunkard's mocking song, is our carefully chosen goal and the object of our holiest longing.

But we must avoid the common fault of pushing the "other world" into the future. It is not future, but present. It parallels our familiar physical world, and the doors between the two worlds are open. "Ye are come," says the writer to the Hebrews (and the tense is plainly present), "unto Mount Zion, and unto the city of the living God, the heavenly Jerusalem, and to an innumerable company of angels, to the general assembly and church of the firstborn, which are written in heaven, and to God the Judge of all, and to the spirits of just men made perfect, and to Jesus the mediator of the new covenant, and to the blood of sprinkling, that speaketh better things than that of Abel." All these things are contrasted with "the mount that might be touched" and "the sound of a trumpet and the voice of words" that might be heard. May we not safely conclude that, as the realities of Mount Sinai were apprehended by the senses, so the realities of Mount Zion are to be grasped by the soul? And this not by any trick of the imagination, but in downright actuality. The soul has eyes with which to see and ears with which to hear. Feeble they may be from long disuse, but by the life-giving touch of Christ alive now and capable of sharpest sight and most sensitive hearing.

As we begin to focus upon God the things of the spirit will take shape before our inner eyes. Obedience to the word of Christ will bring an inward revelation of the Godhead (John 14:21-23). It will give acute perception enabling us to see God even as is promised to the pure in heart. A new God-consciousness will seize upon us and we shall begin to taste and hear and inwardly feel the God who is our life and our all. There will be seen the constant shining of the light that lighteth every man that cometh into the world. More and more, as our faculties grow sharper and more sure, God will become to us the great All, and His Presence the glory and wonder of our lives.

O God, quicken to life every power within me, that I may lay hold on eternal things. Open my eyes that I may see; give me acute spiritual perception; enable me to taste Thee and know that Thou art good. Make heaven more real to me than any earthly thing has ever been. Amen.

14

Restoring the Creator-Creature Relation

Be thou exalted, O God, above the
heavens; let thy glory be above
all the earth.

Ps. 57:5

It is a truism to say that order in nature depends upon right relationships; to achieve harmony each thing must be in its proper position relative to each other thing. In human life it is not otherwise.

I have hinted before in these chapters that the cause of all our human miseries is a radical moral dislocation, an upset in our relation to God and to each other. For whatever else the Fall may have been, it was most certainly a sharp change in man's relation to his Creator. He adopted toward God an altered attitude, and by so doing destroyed the proper Creator-creature relation in which, unknown to him, his true happiness lay. Essentially salvation is the restoration of a right relation between man and his Creator, a bringing back to normal of the Creator-creature relation.

A satisfactory spiritual life will begin with a complete change in relation between God and the sinner; not a judicial change merely, but a conscious and experienced change affecting the sinner's whole nature. The atonement in Jesus' blood makes such a change judicially possible and the working of the Holy Spirit makes it emotionally satisfying. The story of the prodigal son perfectly illustrates this latter phase. He had brought a world of trouble upon himself by forsaking the position which he had properly held as son of his father. At bottom his restoration was nothing more than a re-establishing of the father-son relation which had existed from his birth and had been altered temporarily by his act of sinful rebellion. This story overlooks the legal aspects of redemption, but it makes beautifully clear the experiential aspects of salvation.

In determining relationships we must begin somewhere. There must be somewhere a fixed center against which everything else is measured, where the law of relativity does not enter and we can say "IS" and make no allowances. Such a center is God. When God would make His Name known to mankind He could find no better word than "I AM." When He speaks in the first person He says, "I AM"; when we speak of Him we say, "He is"; when we speak to Him we say, "Thou art." Everyone and everything else measures from that fixed point. "I am that I am," says God, " I change not."

As the sailor locates his position on the sea by "shooting" the sun, so we may get our moral bearings by looking at God. We must begin with God. We are right when and only when we stand in a right position relative to God, and we are wrong so far and so long as we stand in any other position.

Much of our difficulty as seeking Christians stems from our unwillingness to take God as He is and adjust our lives accordingly. We insist upon trying to modify Him and to bring Him nearer to our own image. The flesh whimpers against the rigor of God's inexorable sentence and begs like Agag for a little mercy, a little indulgence of its carnal ways. It is no use. We can get a right start only by accepting God as He is and learning to love Him for what He is. As we go on to know Him better we shall find it a source of unspeakable joy that God is just what He is. Some of the most rapturous moments we know will be those we spend in reverent admiration of the Godhead. In those holy moments the very thought of change in Him will be too painful to endure.

So let us begin with God. Back of all, above all, before all is God; first in sequential order, above in rank and station, exalted in dignity and honor. As the self-existent One He gave being to all things, and all things exist out of Him and for Him. "Thou art worthy, O Lord, to receive glory and honour and power: for thou hast created all things, and for thy pleasure they are and were created."

Every soul belongs to God and exists by His pleasure. God being Who and What He is, and we being who and what we are, the only thinkable relation between us is one of full lordship on His part and complete submission on ours. We owe Him every honor that it is in our power to give Him. Our everlasting grief lies in giving Him anything less.

The pursuit of God will embrace the labor of bringing our total personality into conformity to His. And this not judicially, but actually. I do not here refer to the act of justification by faith in Christ. I speak of a voluntary exalting of God to His proper station over us and a willing surrender of our whole being to the place of worshipful submission which the Creator-creature circumstance makes proper.

The moment we make up our minds that we are going on with this determination to exalt God over all we step out of the world's parade. We shall find ourselves out of adjustment to the ways of the world, and increasingly so as we make progress in the holy way. We shall acquire a new viewpoint; a new and different psychology will be formed within us; a new power will begin to surprise us by its upsurgings and its outgoings.

Our break with the world will be the direct outcome of our changed relation to God. For the world of fallen men does not honor God. Millions call themselves by His

Name, it is true, and pay some token respect to Him, but a simple test will show how little He is really honored among them. Let the average man be put to the proof on the question of who is *above*, and his true position will be exposed. Let him be forced into making a choice between God and money, between God and men, between God and personal amibition, God and self, God and human love, and God will take second place every time. Those other things will be exalted above. However the man may protest, the proof is in the choices he makes day after day throughout his life.

"Be thou exalted" is the language of victorious spiritual experience. It is a little key to unlock the door to great treasures of grace. It is central in the life of God in the soul. Let the seeking man reach a place where life and lips join to say continually "Be thou exalted," and a thousand minor problems will be solved at once. His Christian life ceases to be the complicated thing it had been before and becomes the very essence of simplicity. By the exercise of his will he has set his course, and on that course he will stay as if guided by an automatic pilot. If blown off course for a moment by some adverse wind he will surely return again as by a secret bent of the soul. The hidden motions of the Spirit are working in his favor, and "the stars in their courses" fight for him. He has met his life problem at its center, and everything else must follow along.

Let no one imagine that he will lose anything of human dignity by this voluntary sell-out of his all to his God. He does not by this degrade himself as a man; rather he finds his right place of high honor as one made in the image of his Creator. His deep disgrace lay in his moral derangement, his unnatural usurpation of the place of God. His honor will be proved by restoring again that stolen throne. In exalting God over all he finds his own highest honor upheld.

Anyone who might feel reluctant to surrender his will to

the will of another should remember Jesus' words. "Whosoever committeth sin is the servant of sin." We must of necessity be servant to someone, either to God or to sin. The sinner prides himself on his independence, completely overlooking the fact that he is the weak slave of the sins that rule his members. The man who surrenders to Christ exchanges a cruel slave driver for a kind and gentle Master whose yoke is easy and whose burden is light.

Made as we were in the image of God we scarely find it strange to take again our God as our All. God was our original habitat and our hearts cannot but feel at home when they enter again that ancient and beautiful abode. '

I hope it is clear that there is a logic behind God's claim to pre-eminence. That place is His by every right in earth or heaven. While we take to ourselves the place that is His the whole course of our lives is out of joint. Nothing will or can restore order till our hearts make the great decision: God shall be exalted above.

"Them that honour me I will honour," said God once to a priest of Israel, and that ancient law of the Kingdom stands today unchanged by the passing of time or the changes of dispensation. The whole Bible and every page of history proclaim the perpetuation of that law. "If any man serve me, him will my Father honour," said our Lord Jesus, tying in the old with the new and revealing the essential unity of His ways with men.

Sometimes the best way to see a thing is to look at its opposite. Eli and his sons are placed in the priesthood with the stipulation that they honor God in their lives and ministrations. This they fail to do, and God sends Samuel to announce the consequences. Unknown to Eli this law of reciprocal honor has been all the while secretly working, and now the time has come for judgment to fall. Hophni and Phineas, the degenerate priests, fall in battle, the wife of Hophni dies in childbirth, Israel flees before her enemies, the ark of God is captured by the Philistines and the old man Eli falls backward and dies of a broken neck. Thus stark utter tragedy followed upon Eli's failure to honor God.

Now set over against this almost any Bible character who honestly tried to glorify God in his earthly walk. See how God winked at weaknesses and overlooked failures as He poured upon His servants grace and blessing untold. Let it be Abraham, Jacob, David, Daniel, Elijah or whom you will; honor followed honor as harvest the seed. The man of God set his heart to exalt God above all; God accepted his intention as fact and acted accordingly. Not perfection, but holy intention made the difference.

In our Lord Jesus Christ this law was seen in simple perfection. In His lowly manhood He humbled Himself and glady gave all glory to His Father in heaven. He sought not His own honor, but the honor of God who sent Him. "If I honour myself," He said on one occasion, "my honour is nothing; it is my Father that honoureth me." So far had the proud Pharisees departed from this law that they could not understand one who honored God at his own expense. "I honour my Father," said Jesus to them, "and ye do dishonour me."

Another saying of Jesus, and a most disturbing one, was put in the form of a question, "How can ye believe, which receive honour one of another, and seek not the honour that cometh from God alone?" If I understand this correctly Christ taught here the alarming doctrine that the desire for honor among men made belief impossible. Is this sin at the root of religious unbelief? Could it be that those "intellectual difficulties" which men blame for their inability to believe are but smoke screens to conceal the real cause that lies behind them? Was it this greedy desire for honor from man that made men into Pharisees and Pharisees into Deicides? Is this the secret back of religious self-righteousness and empty worship? I believe it may be. The whole course of the life is upset by failure to put God where He belongs. We exalt ourselves instead of God and the curse follows.

In our desire after God let us keep always in mind that God also hath desire, and His desire is toward the sons of men, and more particularly toward those sons of men who will make the once-for-all decision to exalt Him over all. Such as these are precious to God above all treasures of earth or sea. In them God finds a theater where He can display His exceeding kindness toward us in Christ Jesus. With them God can walk unhindered, toward them He can act like the God He is.

In speaking thus I have one fear; it is that I may convince the mind before God can win the heart. For this God-above-all position is one not easy to take. The mind may approve it while not having the consent of the will to put it into effect. While the imagination races ahead to honor God, the will may lag behind and the man never guess how divided his heart is. The whole man must make the decision before the heart can know any real satisfaction. God wants us all, and He will not rest till He gets us all. No part of the man will do.

Let us pray over this in detail, throwing ourselves at God's feet and meaning everything we say. No one who prays thus in sincerity need wait long for tokens of divine acceptance. God will unveil His glory before His servant's eyes, and He will place all His treasures at the disposal of such a one, for He knows that His honor is safe in such consecrated hands.

O God, be Thou exalted over my possessions. Nothing of earth's treasures shall seem dear unto me if only Thou art glorified in my life. Be Thou exalted over my friendships. I am determined that Thou shalt be above all, though I must stand deserted and alone in the midst of the earth. Be Thou exalted above my comforts. Though it mean the loss of bodily comforts and the carrying of heavy crosses I shall keep my vow made this day before Thee. Be Thou exalted over my reputation. Make me ambitious to please Thee even if as a result I must sink into obscurity and my name be forgotten as a dream. Rise, O Lord, into Thy proper place of honor, above my ambitions, above my likes and dislikes, above my family, my health and even my life itself. Let me decrease that Thou mayest increase, let me sink that Thou mayest rise above. Ride forth upon me as Thou didst ride into Jerusalem mounted upon the humble little beast, a colt, the foal of an ass, and let me hear the children cry to Thee, "Hosanna in the highest."

Excerpts from
The Root of the Righteous

No Regeneration Without Reformation
Faith Is a Perturbing Thing
True Faith Brings Commitment
No Saviourhood Without Lordship

15

No Regeneration Without Reformation

In the Bible the offer of pardon on the part of God is conditioned upon intention to reform on the part of man. There can be no spiritual regeneration till there has been a moral reformation. That this statement requires defense only proves how far from the truth we have strayed.

In our current popular theology pardon depends upon faith alone. The very word *reform* has been banished from among the sons of the Reformation!

We often hear the declaration, "I do not preach reformation; I preach regeneration." Now we recognize this as being the expression of a commendable revolt against the insipid and unscriptural doctrine of salvation by human effort. But the declaration as it stands contains real error, for it opposes reformation to regeneration. Actually the two are never opposed to each other in sound Bible theology. The not-reformation-but-regeneration doctrine incorrectly presents us with an either-or; either you take reformation or you take regeneration. This is inaccurate. The fact is that on this subject we are presented not with an either-or, but with a both-and. The converted man is both reformed and regenerated. And unless the sinner is willing to reform his way of living he will never know the inward experience of regeneration. This is the vital truth which has gotten lost under the leaves in popular evangelical theology.

The idea that God will pardon a rebel who has not given up his rebellion is contrary both to the Scriptures and to common sense. How horrible to contemplate a church full of persons who have been pardoned but who still love sin and hate the ways of righteousness. And how much more horrible to think of heaven as filled with sinners who had not repented nor changed their way of living.

A familiar story will illustrate this. The governor of one of our states was visiting the state prison incognito. He fell into conversation with a personable young convict and felt a secret wish to pardon him. "What would you do," he asked casually, "if you were lucky enough to obtain a pardon?" The convict, not knowing to whom he was speaking, snarled his reply: "If I ever get out of this place, the first thing I'll do is to cut the throat of the judge who sent me here." The governor broke off the conversation and withdrew from the cell. The convict stayed on in prison. To pardon a man who had not reformed would be to let loose another killer upon society. That kind of pardon would not only be foolish, it would be downright immoral.

The promise of pardon and cleansing is always associated in the Scriptures with the command to repent. The widely-used text in Isaiah, "Though your sins be as scarlet, they shall be as white as snow; though they be red like crimson, they shall be as wool," is organically united to the verses that precede it: "Wash you, make you clean; put away the evil of your doings from before mine eyes; cease to do evil; learn to do well; seek judgment, relieve the oppressed, judge the fatherless, plead for the widow." What does this teach but radical reformation of life before there can be any expectation of pardon? To divorce the words from each other is to do violence to the Scriptures and to convict ourselves of deceitfully handling the truth.

I think there is little doubt that the teaching of salvation without repentance has lowered the moral standards of the Church and produced a multitude of deceived religious professors who erroneously believe themselves to be saved when in fact they are still in the gall of bitterness and the bond of iniquity. And to see such persons actually seeking the deeper life is a grim and disillusioning sight. Yet our altars are sometimes filled with seekers who are crying with Simon, "Give me this power," when the moral groundwork has simply not been laid for it. The whole thing must be acknowledged as a clear victory for the devil, a victory he could never have enjoyed if unwise teachers had not made it possible by preaching the evil doctrine of regeneration apart from reformation.

16

Faith Is a Perturbing Thing

"Faith," said the early Lutherans, "is a perturbing thing."

To Martin Luther goes the credit under God for having rediscovered the Biblical doctrine of justification by faith. Luther's emphasis upon faith as the only way into peace of heart and deliverance from sin gave a new impulse of life to the decadent Church and brought about the Reformation. That much is history. It is not a matter of opinion but of simple fact. Anyone can check it.

But something has happened to the doctrine of justification by faith as Luther taught it. What has happened is not so easily discovered. It is not a matter of simple fact, a plain yes or no, an obvious black or white. It is more elusive than that, and very much more difficult to come at; but what has happened is so serious and so vital that it has changed or is in the process of changing the whole evangelical outlook. If it continues it may well turn Christianity inside out and put for the faith of our fathers something else entirely. And the whole spiritual revolution will be so gradual and so innocent appearing that it will hardly be noticed. Anyone who fights it will be accused of jousting against windmills like Don Quixote.

The faith of Paul and Luther was a revolutionizing thing. It upset the whole life of the individual and made him into another person altogether. It laid hold on the life and brought it under obedience to Christ. It took up its cross and followed along after Jesus with no intention of going back. It said good-bye to its old friends as certainly as Elijah when he stepped into the fiery chariot and went away in the whirlwind. It has a finality about it. It snapped shut on a man's heart like a trap; it captured the man and made him from that moment forward a happy love-servant of his Lord. It turned earth into a desert and drew heaven within sight of the believing soul. It realigned all life's actions and brought them into accord with the will of God. It set its possessor on a pinnacle of truth from which spiritual vantage point he viewed everything that came into his field of experience. It made him little and God big and Christ unspeakably dear. All this and more happened to a man when he received the faith that justifies.

Came the revolution, quietly, certainly, and put another construction upon the word "faith." Little by little the whole meaning of the word shifted from what it had been to what it is now. And so insidious was the change that hardly a voice has been raised to warn against it. But the tragic consequences are all around us.

Faith now means no more than passive moral acquiescence in the Word of God and the cross of Jesus. To exercise it we have only to rest on one knee and nod our heads in agreement with the instructions of a personal worker intent upon saving our soul. The general effect is much the same as that which men feel after a visit to a good and wise doctor. They come back from such a visit feeling extra good, withal smiling just a little sheepishly to think how many fears they had entertained about their health when actually there was nothing wrong with them. They just needed a rest.

Such a faith as this does not perturb people. It comforts them. It does not put their hip out of joint so that they halt upon their thigh; rather it teachers them deep breathing exercises and improves their posture. The face of their ego is washed and their self-confidence is rescued from discouragement. All this they gain, but they do not get a new name as Jacob did, nor do they limp into the eternal sunlight. "As he passed over Penuel the sun rose upon him." That was Jacob—rather, that was Israel, for the sun did not shine much upon Jacob. It was ashamed to. But it loved to rest upon the head of the man whom God had transformed.

This generation of Christians must hear again the doctrine of the perturbing quality of faith. People must be told that the Christian religion is not something they can trifle with. The faith of Christ will command or it will have nothing to do with a man. It will not yield to experimentation. Its power cannot reach any man who is secretly keeping an escape route open in case things get too tough for him. The only man who can be sure he has true Bible faith is the one who has put himself in a position where he cannot go back. His faith has resulted in an everlasting and irrevocable committal, and however strongly he may be tempted he always replies, "Lord, to whom shall we go? thou hast the words of eternal life."

17

True Faith Brings Commitment

To many Christians Christ is little more than an idea, or at best an ideal. He is not a fact. Millions of professed believers talk as if He were real and act as if He were not. And always our actual position is to be discovered by the way we act, not by the way we talk.

We can prove our faith by our commitment to it, and in no other way. Any belief that does not command the one who holds it is not a real belief; it is a pseudo belief only. And it might shock some of us profoundly if we were brought suddenly face to face with our beliefs and forced to test them in the fires of practical living.

Many of us Christians have become extremely skillful in arranging our lives so as to admit the truth of Christianity without being embarrassed by its implications. We arrange things so that we can get on well enough without divine aid, while at the same time ostensibly seeking it. We boast in the Lord but watch carefully that we never get caught depending on Him. "The heart is deceitful above all things, and desperately wicked: who can know it?"

Pseudo faith always arranges a way out to serve in case God fails it. Real faith knows only one way and gladly allows itself to be stripped of any second way or makeshift substitutes. For true faith, it is either God or total collapse. And not sense Adam first stood up on the earth has God failed a single man or woman who trusted Him.

The man of pseudo faith will fight for his verbal creed but refuse flatly to allow himself to get into a predicament where his future must depend upon that creed being true. He always provides himself with secondary ways of escape so he will have a way out if the roof caves in.

What we need very badly these days is a company of Christians who are prepared to trust God as completely now as they know they must do at the last day. For each of us the time is surely coming when we shall have nothing but God. Health and wealth and friends and hiding places will all be swept away and we shall have only God. To the man of pseudo faith that is a terrifying thought, but to real faith it is one of the most comforting thoughts the heart can entertain.

It would be a tragedy indeed to come to the place where we have no other but God and find that we had not really been trusting God during the days of our earthly sojourn. It would be better to invite God now to remove every false trust, to disengage our hearts from all secret hiding places and to bring us out into the open where we can discover for ourselves whether or not we actually trust Him. That is a harsh cure for our troubles, but it is a sure one. Gentler cures may be too weak to do the work. And time is running out on us.

18

No Saviourhood Without Lordship

We must never underestimate the ability of human beings to get themselves tangled up.

Mankind appears to have a positive genius for twisting truth until it ceases to be truth and becomes downright falsehood. By overemphasizing in one place and under-emphasizing in another the whole pattern of truth may be so altered that a completely false view results without our being aware of it.

This fact was brought forcibly to mind recently by hearing again the discredited doctrine of a divided Christ so widely current a few years ago and still accepted in many religious circles. It goes like this: Christ is both Saviour and Lord. A sinner may be saved by accepting Him as Saviour without yielding to Him as Lord. The practical outworking of this doctrine is that the evangelist presents and the seeker accepts a divided Christ. We have all heard the tearful plea made to persons already saved to accept Christ as Lord and thus enter into the victorious life.

Almost all deeper life teaching is based upon this fallacy, but because it contains a germ of truth its soundness is not questioned. Anyway, it is extremely simple and quite popular, and in addition to these selling points it is also ready-made for both speaker and hearer and requires no thinking by either. So sermons embodying this heresy are freely preached, books are written and songs composed, all saying the same thing; and all saying the wrong thing, except, as I have said, for a feeble germ of truth lying inert at the bottom.

Now, it seems odd that none of these teachers ever noticed that the only true object of saving faith is none other than Christ Himself; not the "saviourhood" of Christ nor the "lordship" of Christ, but Christ Himself. God does not offer salvation to the one who will believe on one of the offices of Christ, nor is an office of Christ ever presented as an object of faith. Neither are we exhorted to believe on the atonement, nor on the cross, nor on the priesthood of the Saviour. All of these are embodied in the person of Christ, but they are never separated nor is one ever isolated from the rest. Much less are we permitted to accept one of Christ's offices and reject another. The notion that we are so permitted is a modern day heresy, I repeat, and like every heresy it has had evil consequences among Christians. No heresy is ever entertained with impunity. We pay in practical failure for our theoretical errors.

It is altogether doubtful whether any man can be saved who comes to Christ for His help but with no intention to obey Him. Christ's saviourhood is forever united to His lordship. Look at the Scriptures: "If thou shalt confess with thy mouth the Lord Jesus, and shalt believe in thine heart that God hath raised him from the dead, thou shalt be saved . . . for the same Lord over all is rich unto all that call upon him. For whosoever shall call upon the name of the Lord shall be saved" (Rom. 10:9–13). There the *Lord* is the object of faith for salvation. And when the Philippian jailer asked the way to be saved, Paul replied, "Believe on the Lord Jesus Christ, and thou shalt be saved" (Acts 16:31). He did not tell him to believe on the Saviour with the thought that he could later take up the matter of His lordship and settle it at his own convenience. To Paul there could be no division of offices. Christ must be Lord or He will not be Saviour.

There is no intention here to teach that the earnest believer may not go on to explore ever-increasing meanings in Christ, nor do we hold that our first saving contact with Christ brings perfect knowledge of all He is to us. The contrary is true. Ages upon ages will hardly be long enough to allow us to experience all the riches of His grace. As we discover new meanings in his titles and make them ours we will grow in the knowledge of our Lord and in personal appreciation of the multifold offices He fills and the many forms of love He wears exalted on His throne. That is the truth which has been twisted out of shape and reduced to impotence by the doctrine that we can believe on His saviourhood while rejecting His lordship.

19

Why the Holy Spirit Is Given

A generation ago the work of the Holy Spirit in the life of the believer was neatly reduced by certain Bible teachers to one thing: to impart power for service.

In the first quarter of the present century the phrase "power for service" occurred everywhere in the literature of evangelical Christianity, and one gets the distinct impression that it was meant to serve as a Biblical reason for the presenece of the Holy Spirit in the church other than that advanced by the charismatic sects which about that time were going big in varius parts of the world, especially in the United States. These claimed that they had returned to basic New Testament Christianity and offered as proof the presence of the Spirit's gifts among them, with particular, one might say exclusive, emphasis on the gift of tongues. This teaching was accompanied by a great outburst of emotionalism. Those who had the experience enjoyed it immensely and the onlookers could not but be deeply affected by this demonstration of joy.

The more staid members of the evangelical community could not go along with the emotionalism of the Pentecostalists nor with the obvious lack of balance in their theology and lack of responsibility in their general conduct. But the matter of the Spirit had to be dealt with. The popular Bible teachers came up with the "power for service" doctrine and a lot of good people were greatly relieved. According to this counter-doctrine, the infilling of the Spirit is necessary and altogether to be desired, but for reasons other than those advanced by the Pentecostalists. The one great work of the Spirit in the life of the believer, they said, is to impart "power for service." Thus it is not emotional or charismatic but practical. The Christian is weak and the Spirit is given to make him strong so that he can serve effectively. This view was supported by Acts 1:8: "Ye shall receive power, after that the Holy Ghost is come upon you: and ye shall be witnesses unto me."

Now I have often tried to make the point that truths that are compelled to stand alone never stand straight and are not likely to stand long. Truth is one but truths are many. Scriptural truths are interlocking and interdependent. A trust is rarely valid in isolation. A statement may be true in its relation to other truths and less than true when separated from them. "The truth, the whole truth, and nothing but the truth" is good not only for a court of law but for the pulpit, the classroom and the prayer chamber as well.

To teach that the filling with the Holy Spirit is given to the Christian to provide "power for service" is to teach truth, but not the whole truth. Power for service is but one effect of the experience, and I do not hesitate to say that it is the least of several effects. It is least for the very reason that it touches service, presumably service to mankind; and contrary to the popular belief, "to serve this present age" is not the Christian's first duty nor the chief end of man.

As I have stated elsewhere, the two great verbs that dominate the life of man are *be* and *do*. What a man *is* comes first in the sight of God. What he does is determined by what he is, so *is* is of first importance always. The modern notion that we are "saved to serve," while true, is true only in a wider context, and as understood by busy Christians today it is not true at all.

Redemption became necessary not because of what men were doing only, but because of what they were. Not human conduct alone had gone wrong but human nature as well; apart from the moral defect in human nature no evil conduct would have occurred. Fallen men acted in accord with what they were. Their hearts dictated their deeds. "And God saw that the wickedness of man was great in the earth." That much any moral being could have seen. But God saw more; He saw the cause of man's wicked ways, and that "every imagination of the thoughts of his heart was only evil continually." The stream of human conduct flows out of a fountain polluted by evil thoughts and imaginations.

To purge the stream it was necessary to purify the fountain; and to reform human conduct it is necessary to regenerate human nature. The fundamental *be* must be sanctified if we would have a righteous *do,* for being and doing are related as cause and effect, as father and son.

The primary work of the Holy Spirit is to restore the lost soul to intimate fellowship with God through the washing of regeneration. To accomplish this He first reveals Christ to the penitent heart (I Cor. 12:3). He then goes on to illumine the newborn soul with brighter rays from the face of Christ (John 14:26; 16:13–15) and leads the willing heart into depths and heights of divine knowledge and communion. Remember, we know Christ only as the Spirit enables us and we have only as much of Him as the Holy Spirit imparts.

God wants worshipers before workers; indeed the only acceptable workers are those who have learned the lost art of worship. It is inconceivable that a sovereign and holy God should be so hard up for workers that He would press into service anyone who had been empowered regardless of his moral qualifications. The very stones would praise Him if the need arose and a thousand legions of angels would leap to His will.

Gifts and power for service the Spirit surely desires to impart; but holiness and spiritual worship come first.

20

The Divine Indwelling

The doctrine of the divine indwelling is one of the most important in the New Testament, and its meaning for the individual Christian is precious beyond all description. To neglect it is to suffer serious loss. The apostle Paul prayed for the Ephesian Christians that Christ might dwell in their hearts by faith. Surely it takes faith of a more than average vitality to grasp the full implications of this great truth.

Two facts join to make the doctrine difficult to accept: the supreme greatness of God and the utter sinfulness of man. Those who think poorly of God and well of themselves may chatter idly of "the deity within," but the man who trembles before the high and lofty One that inhabiteth eternity, whose name is Holy, the man who knows the depth of his own sin, will detect a moral incongruity in the teaching that One so holy should dwell in the heart of one so vile.

But however incongruous it may appear to be, in the Holy Scriptures it is taught so fully that it cannot be overlooked and so plainly that it can hardly be misunderstood. "If a man love me," said our Lord Jesus Christ, "he will keep my words: and my Father will love him, and we will come unto him, and make our abode with him" (John 14:23). That this abiding is *within the man* is shown by these words: "At that day ye shall know that I am in my Father, and ye in me, and I in you" (vs. 20). Christ said of the Holy Spirit: "He ... shall be in you" (vs. 17), and in His great prayer in John 17 our Lord twice used the words "I in them."

The truth of the divine indwelling is developed more fully in the epistles of Paul. "Know ye not that ye are the temple of God, and that the Spirit of God dwelleth in you?... For the temple of God is holy, which temple ye are" (I Cor. 3:16, 17). And again (I Cor. 6:19), "What? know ye not that your body is the temple of the Holy Ghost which is in you, which ye have of God, and ye are not your own?"

Without question, the teaching of the New Testament is that the very God Himself inhabits the nature of His true children. How this can be I do not know, but neither do I know how my soul inhabits my body. Paul called this wonder of the indwelling God a rich mystery: "Christ in you, the hope of glory." And if the doctrine involved a contradiction or even an impossibility we must still believe what the mouth of the Lord has spoken. "Yea, let God be true, but every man a liar" (Rom. 3:4).

The spiritual riches lying buried in this truth are so vast that they are worth any care or effort we may give to their recovery. Yet we are not concerned primarily with the theology or metaphysics embodied here. We want to know the reality of it. What does the truth mean to us in practical outworking? What does it have for a serious-minded Christian compelled to live in a dark and godless world? As Paul would say, "Much every way."

God does not dwell passively in His people; He *wills* and *works* in them (Phil. 2:13); and remember, wherever He is, God always acts like Himself. He will do in us whatever His holy nature moves Him to do; and unless He is hindered by our resistance He will act in us precisely as He acts in heaven. Only an unsanctified human will can prevent Him.

Without doubt we hinder God greatly by our willfulness and our unbelief. We fail to cooperate with the holy impulses of the inliving Spirit; we go contrary to His will as it is revealed in the Scriptures, either because we have not taken time to discover what the Bible teaches or because we do not approve it when we do.

This contest between the indwelling Deity and our own fallen propensities occupies a large place in New Testament theology. But the warfare need not continue indefinitely. Christ has made full provision for our deliverance from the bondage of the flesh. A frank and realistic presentation of the whole thing is set forth in Romans six and seven, and in the eighth chapter a triumphant solution is discovered: It is, briefly, through a spiritual cruxifixion with Christ followed by resurrection and an infusion of the Holy Spirit.

Once the heart is freed from its contrary impulses, Christ within becomes a wondrous experiential fact. The surrendered heart has no more controversy with God, so He can live in us congenial and uninhibited. Then He thinks His own thoughts in us: thoughts about ourselves, about Himself, about sinners and saints and babes and harlots; thoughts about the church, about sin and judgment and hell and heaven. And He thinks about us and Himself and His love for us and our love for Him; and He woos us to Himself as a bridegroom woos his bride.

Yet there is nothing formal or automatic about His operations within us. We are personalities and we are engaged with personality. We are intelligent and have wills of our own. We can, so to speak, stand outside of ourselves and discipline ourselves into accord with the will of God. We can commune with our own hearts upon our beds and be still. We can talk to our God in the night watches. We can learn what He wants us to be, and pray and work to prepare Him a habitation.

And what kind of habitation pleases God? What must our natures be like before He can feel at home within us? He asks nothing but a pure heart and a single mind. He asks no rich paneling, no rugs from the Orient, no art treasures from afar. He desires but sincerity, transparency, humility and love. He will see to the rest.

21

We Are Saved **To** *as well as* **From**

The evangelical church today is in the awkward position of being wrong while it is right, and a little preposition makes the difference.

I think there can be no question but that if we let the Bible decide right and wrong the evangelicals are right in their creedal position. Even the skeptic, H. L. Mencken, said, "If the Bible is true, the fundamentalists are right." He did not grant the truth of the Bible, but he was sharp enough to see that the basic doctrines taught by fundamentalists were identical with those taught by the Bible.

One place where we are wrong while we are right is in the relative stress we lay upon the prepositions *to* and *from* when they follow the word *saved*. For a long generation we have been holding the letter of truth while at the same time we have been moving away from it in spirit because we have been preoccupied with what we are saved *from* rather than what we have been saved *to*.

The right relative importance of the two concepts is set forth by Paul in his first epistle to the Thessalonians: "Ye turned to God from idols to serve the living and true God; and to wait for his Son from heaven."

The Christian is saved from his past sins. With these he simply has nothing more to do; they are among the things to be forgotten as the night is forgotten at the dawning of the day. He is also saved from the wrath to come. With this

also he has nothing to do. It exists, but not for him. Sin and
wrath have a cause and effect relationship, and because for
the Christian sin is canceled wrath is canceled also. The
from's of the Christian life concern negatives, and to be
engrossed in them is to live in a state of negation. Yet that
is where many earnest believers live most of the time.

We are not called to fellowship with nonexistence. We
are called to things that exist in truth, to positive things,
and it is as we become occupied with these that health
comes to the soul. Spiritual life cannot feed on negatives.
The man who is constantly reciting the evils of his uncon-
verted days is looking in the wrong direction. He is like a
man trying to run a race while looking back over his shoul-
der.

What the Christian used to be is altogether the least important thing about him. What he is yet to be is all that
should concern him. He may occasionally, as Paul sometimes did, remember to his own shame the life he once
lived; but that should be only a quick glance; it is never to
be a fixed gaze. Our long permanent look is on God and
the glory that shall be revealed.

What we are saved *from* and what we are saved *to* bear
the same relation to each other as a serious illness and
recovered health. The physician should stand between
these two opposites to save from one and restore to the
other. Once the great sickness is cured the memory of it
should be thrust out onto the margin of the mind to grow
fainter and weaker as it retreats farther away; and the for-
tunate man whose health has been restored should go on
to use his new strength to accomplish something useful for
mankind.

Yet many persons permit their sick bodies to condition
their mental stuff so that after the body has gotten well
they still retain the old feeling of chronic invalidism they
had before. They are recovered, true enough, but not *to*
anything. We have but to imagine a group of such persons
testifying every Sunday about their late illnesses and sing-

Danita
loves you.

I
LOVE YOU

Have
a
happy
day.

Shirley

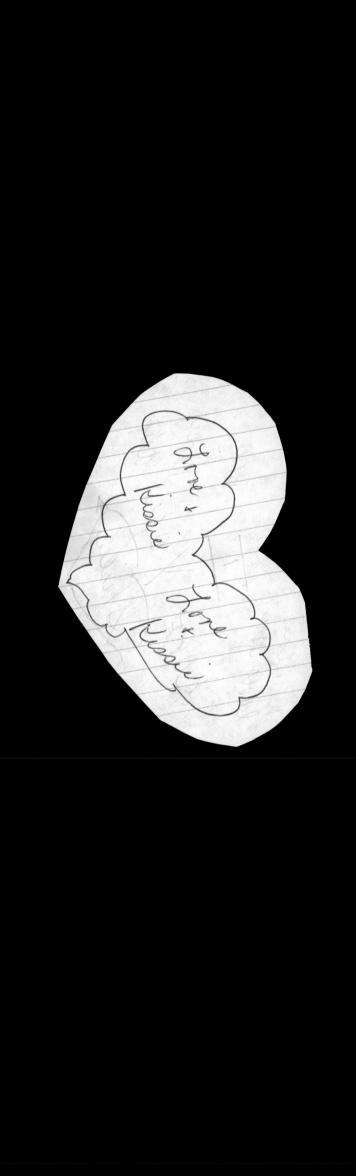

ing plaintive songs about them and we have a pretty fair picture of many gatherings among Christians today.

There is an art of forgetting, and every Christian should become skilled in it. Forgetting the things which are behind is a positive necessity if we are to become more than mere babes in Christ. If we cannot trust God to have dealt effectually with our past we may as well throw in the sponge now and have it over with. Fifty years of grieving over our sins cannot blot out their guilt. But if God has indeed pardoned and cleansed us, then we should count it done and waste no more time in sterile lamentations.

And thank God this sudden obliteration of our familiar past does not leave us with a vacuum. Far from it. Into the empty world vacated by our sins and failures rushes the blessed Spirit of God, bringing with Him everything new. New life, new hope, new enjoyments, new interests, new purposeful toil, and best of all a new and satisfying object toward which to direct our soul's enraptured gaze. God now fills the recovered garden, and we may without fear walk and commune with Him in the cool of the day.

Right here is where the weakness of much current Christianity lies. We have not learned where to lay our emphasis. Particularly we have not understood that we are saved to know God, to enter His wonder-filled Presence through the new and living way and remain in that Presence forever. We are called to an everlasting preoccupation with God. The Triune God with all of His mystery and majesty is ours and we are His, and eternity will not be long enough to experience all that He is of goodness, holiness and truth.

In heaven they rest not day or night in their ecstatic worship of the Godhead. We profess to be headed for that place; shall we not begin now to worship on earth as we shall do in heaven?

22

The Need for Divine Illumination

Spiritual truths differ from natural truths both in their constitution and in the manner of their apprehension by us.

Natural truths can be learned by us regardless of our moral or spiritual condition. The truths of the natural sciences, for instance, can be grasped by anyone of normal intelligence regardless of whether he is a good man or a scoundrel. There is no relation between, say, chastity and logic, or between kindness and oceanography. In like manner a sufficient degree of mental vigor is all that is required to grasp philosophical propositions. A man may study philosophy for a lifetime, teach it, write books about it, and be all the while proud, covetous and thoroughly dishonest in his private dealings.

The same thing may be said of theology. A man need not be godly to learn theology. Indeed I wonder whether there is anything taught in any seminary on earth that could not be learned by a brigand or a swindler as well as by a consecrated Christian. While I have no doubt that the majority of theological students live far better than average lives, yet it should be kept in mind that they can easily get their lessons without living any better than is absolutely required to stay in the institution.

It does not strain my imagination to think of Judas Iscariot as coming out of school with a Th.B., if such a thing had been offered in his day. There is simply no necessary relation between the studies engaged in by students in a divinity school and the state of the students' hearts. Anything that is taught under the heading of hamartiology, soteriology, eschatology, pneumatology or any of the rest may be grasped as easily by a sinner as by a saint. And certainly it takes no great degree of sanctity to learn Hebrew and Greek.

Surely God has that to say to the pure in heart which He cannot say to the man of sinful life. But what He has to say is not theological, it is spiritual; and right there lies the weight of my argument. Spiritual truths cannot be received in the ordinary way of nature. "The natural man receiveth not the things of the Spirit of God: for they are foolishness unto him: neither can he know them, because they are spiritually discerned." So wrote the apostle Paul to the believers at Corinth.

Our Lord referred to this kind of Spirit-enlightened knowledge many times. To Him it was the fruit of a divine illumination, not contrary to but altogether beyond mere intellectual light. The fourth Gospel is full of this idea; indeed the idea is so important to the understanding of John's Gospel that anyone who denies it might as well give up trying to grasp our Lord's teachings as given by the apostle John. And the same idea is found in John's First Epistle, making that epistle extremely difficult to understand but also making it one of the most beautiful and rewarding of all the epistles of the New Testament when its teachings are spiritually discerned.

The necessity for spiritual illumination before we can grasp spiritual truths is taught throughout the entire New Testament and is altogether in accord with the teachings of the Psalms, the Proverbs and the Prophets. The Old Testament Apocrypha agrees with the Scriptures here, and while the Apocryphal books are not to be received as divinely inspired, they are useful as showing how the best minds of ancient Israel thought about this matter of divine truth and how it is received into the human heart.

The New Testament draws a sharp line between the natural mind and the mind that has been touched by divine fire. When Peter made his good confession, "Thou art the Christ, the Son of the living God," our Lord replied, "Blessed art thou, Simon Bar-jona: for flesh and blood hath not revealed it unto thee, but my Father which is in heaven." And Paul expresses much the same thing when he says, "No man can say that Jesus is the Lord, but by the Holy Ghost."

The sum of what I am saying is that there is an illumination, divinely bestowed, without which theological truth is information and nothing more. While this illumination is never given apart from theology, it is entirely possible to have theology without the illumination. This results in what has been called "dead orthodoxy," and while there may be some who deny that it is possible to be both orthodox and dead at the same time I am afraid experience proves that it is.

Revivals, as they have appeared at various times among the churches of the past, have been essentially a quickening of the spiritual life of persons already orthodox. The revivalist, as long as he exercised his ministry as a revivalist, did not try to teach doctrine. His one object was to bring about a quickening of the churches which while orthodox in creed were devoid of spiritual life. When he went beyond this he was something else than a revivalist. Revival can come only to those who know truth. When the inner meaning of familiar doctrines suddenly flashes in upon the heart of a Christian the revival for him has already begun. It may go on to be much more than this but it can never be less.

23

The Sanctification of Our Minds

Thinking is a kind of living. To think and to be aware that we think is to be conscious; life without consciousness is but a shadow of life, having no meaning and being of no value to the individual. Our thoughts are the product of our thinking, and since these are of such vast importance to us it is imperative that we learn how to think rightly.

I am not concerned here with that kind of profound cerebration known as "heavy thinking." Few of us have the intellectual equipment to enable us, or the will power to compel us, to engage in such heroic mental exercise. I am dealing here with that kind of thinking done by every normal person every waking moment from birth to death.

After all, it is not our heavy thinking that shapes our characters, but the quiet attention of the mind to the surrounding world day after day throughout our lives. Men are influenced more by their common, everyday thinking than by any rare intellectual feat such as writing a great poem or painting a famous picture. Feats of thinking may create reputation, but habits of thinking create character. The incredible mental accomplishments of an Einstein, for instance, had almost nothing to do with the kind of human being he was; the constant, undramatic, moment-by-moment interplay of his mind with his environment, on the other hand, had almost everything to do with it.

We all live in two environments, the one being the world

around us, the other our thoughts about that world. The larger world cannot affect us directly; it must be mediated to us by our thoughts, and will be to us at last only what we allow it to be.

Three men walking side by side may yet be inhabiting three different worlds. Imagine a poet, a naturalist and a lumberman traveling together through a forest. The poet's mind races back over the centuries to the time when the mighty trees now towering above him were but beginning to appear as tiny green shoots out of the gray earth. He dreams of the mighty of the world who then wore crowns and swayed empires, but who have long ago passed from this earthly scene and been forgotten by everyone but a few historians.

The naturalist's world is smaller and more detailed. He hears the sweet, hardly audible bird song that floats among the branches and seeks to discover the hidden singer; he knows what kind of moss it is that clings to the base of the centuries-old trees; he seeks what the others miss, the fresh claw marks on the bark of a tree, and knows that a bear has recently passed that way.

The lumberman's world is smaller still. He is concerned neither with history nor nature but with lumber. He judges the diameter and height of the tree, and by quick calculation determines how much it will bring on the market. His world is the dull world of commerce. He sees nothing beyond it.

It is obvious that one external world has been turned into three internal worlds by the thinking of the three men. External things and events are the raw material only; the finished product is whatever the mind makes of these. Judas Iscariot and John the Beloved lived in the same world, but how differently they interpreted it. The same may be said of Cain and Abel, Esau and Jacob, Saul and David. From these we learn that circumstances do not make men; it is their reaction to circumstances that determines what kind of men they will be.

What then can we Christians do? The answer is, "Let this mind be in you, which was also in Christ Jesus." "Know ye not your own selves, how that Jesus Christ is in you, except ye be reprobates?" The mental stuff of the Christian can be and should be modified and conditioned by the Spirit of Christ which indwells his nature. God wills that we think His thoughts after Him. The Spirit-filled, prayerful Christian actually possesses the mind of Christ, so that his reactions to the external world are the same as Christ's. He thinks about people and things just as Christ does. All life becomes to him the raw nectar which the Spirit within him turns into the honey of paradise.

Yet this is not automatic. To do His gracious work God must have the intelligent cooperation of His people. If we would think God's thoughts we must learn to think continually of God. "God thinks continuously of each one of us as if He had no one but ourselves," said Francois Malaval; "it is therefore no more than just if we think continuously of Him, as if we had no one but Himself."

We must think of the surrounding world of people and things against the background of our thoughts of God. The experienced Christian will never think of anything directly; his thoughts go first to God and from God out to His creation. His thoughts, like the angels of Jacob's ladder, ascend and descend, but ever God stands above them presiding over all.

To be heavenly-minded we must think heavenly thoughts. "So let us return to ourselves, brothers, . . . for it is impossible for us to be reconciled and united with God if we do not first return to ourselves, . . . striving constantly to keep attention on the kingdom of heaven which is within us."

So wrote Nicephorus, a father of the Greek Orthodox Church, in the fourteenth century, and nothing since has changed. God must have all our thoughts if we would experience the sanctification of our minds.

Excerpts from
Of God and Men

We Need Men of God Again
The Cross Does Interfere
Each His Own Cross
Religion Should Produce Action

24

We Need Men of God Again

The church at this moment needs men, the right kind of men, bold men. The talk is that we need revival, that we need a new baptism of the Spirit—and God knows we must have both; but God will not revive mice. He will not fill rabbits with the Holy Ghost.

We languish for men who feel themselves expendable in the warfare of the soul, who cannot be frightened by threats of death because they have already died to the allurements of this world. Such men will be free from the compulsions that control weaker men. They will not be forced to do things by the squeeze of circumstances; their only compulsion will come from within—or from above.

This kind of freedom is necessary if we are to have prophets in our pulpits again instead of mascots. These free men will serve God and mankind from motives too high to be understood by the rank and file of religious retainers who today shuttle in and out of the sanctuary. They will make no decisions out of fear, take no course out of a desire to please, accept no service for financial considerations, perform no religious act out of mere custom; nor will they allow themselves to be influenced by the love of publicity or the desire for reputation.

Much that the church—even the evangelical church—is doing these days she is doing because she is afraid not to. Ministerial associations take up projects for no higher reason than that they are being scared into it. Whatever their ear-to-the-ground, fear-inspired reconnoitering leads them to believe the world expects them to do they will be doing come next Monday morning with all kinds of trumped-up zeal and show of godliness. The pressure of public opinion calls these prophets, not the voice of Jehovah.

The true church has never sounded out public expectations before launching her crusades. Her leaders heard from God and went ahead wholly independent of popular support or the lack of it. They knew their Lord's will and did it, and their people followed them—sometimes to triumph, oftener to insults and public persecution—and their sufficient reward was the satisfaction of being right in a wrong world.

Another characteristic of the true prophet has been love. The free man who has learned to hear God's voice and dared to obey it has felt the moral burden that broke the hearts of the Old Testament prophets, crushed the soul of our Lord Jesus Christ and wrung streams of tears from the eyes of the apostles.

The free man has never been a religious tyrant, nor has he sought to lord it over God's heritage. It is fear and lack of self-assurance that has led men to try to crush others under their feet. These have had some interest to protect, some position to secure, so they have demanded subjection from their followers as a guarantee of their own safety. But the free man—never; he has nothing to protect, no ambition to pursue and no enemy to fear. For that reason he is completely careless of his standing among men. If they follow him, well and good; if not, he loses nothing that he holds dear; but whether he is accepted or rejected he will go on loving his people with sincere devotion. And only death can silence his tender intercession for them.

Yes, if evangelical Christianity is to stay alive she must have men again, the right kind of men. She must repudiate the weaklings who dare not speak out, and she must seek in prayer and much humility the coming again of men of the stuff prophets and martyrs are made of. God will hear the cries of His people as He heard the cries of Israel in Egypt. And He will send deliverance by sending deliverers. It is His way among men.

And when the deliverers come—reformers, revivalists, prophets—they will be men of God and men of courage. They will have God on their side because they will be careful to stay on God's side. They will be co-workers with Christ and instruments in the hand of the Holy Ghost. Such men will be baptized with the Spirit indeed, and through their labors He will baptize others and send the long delayed revival.

25

The Cross Does Interfere

"Things have come to a pretty pass," said a famous Englishman testily, "when religion is permitted to interfere with our private lives."

To which we may reply that things have come to a worse pass when an intelligent man living in a Protestant country could make such a remark. Had this man never read the New Testament? Had he never heard of Stephen? or Paul? or Peter? Had he never thought about the millions who followed Christ cheerfully to violent death, sudden or lingering, because they *did* allow their religion to interfere with their private lives?

But we must leave this man to his conscience and his Judge and look into our own hearts. Maybe he but expressed openly what some of us feel secretly. Just how radically has our religion interfered with the neat pattern of our own lives? Perhaps we had better answer that question first.

I have long believed that a man who spurns the Christian faith outright is more respected before God and the heavenly powers than the man who pretends to religion but refuses to come under its total domination. The first is an overt enemy, the second a false friend. It is the latter who will be spued out of the mouth of Christ; and the reason is not hard to understand.

One picture of a Christian is a man carrying a cross. "If

any man will come after me, let him deny himself, and take up his cross, and follow me." The man with a cross no longer controls his destiny; he lost control when he picked up his cross. That cross immediately became to him an all-absorbing interest, an overwhelming interference. No matter what he may desire to do, there is but one thing he *can* do; that is, move on toward the place of crucifixion.

The man who will not brook interference is under no compulsion to follow Christ. "If any man will," said our Lord, and thus freed every man and placed the Christian life in the realm of voluntary choice.

Yet no man can escape interference. Law, duty, hunger, accident, natural disasters, illness, death, all intrude into his plans, and in the long run there is nothing he can do about it. Long experience with the rude necessities of life has taught men that these interferences will be thrust upon them sooner or later, so they learn to make what terms they can with the inevitable. They learn how to stay within the narrow circular rabbit path where the least interference is to be found. The bolder ones may challenge the world, enlarge the circle somewhat and so increase the number of their problems, but no one invites trouble deliberately. Human nature is not built that way.

Truth is a glorious but hard mistress. She never consults, bargains or compromises. She cries from the top of the high places, "Receive my instruction, and not silver; and knowledge rather than choice gold." After that, every man is on his own. He may accept or refuse, receive or set at naught as he pleases; and there will be no attempt at coercion, though the man's whole destiny is at stake.

Let a man become enamored of Eternal Wisdom and set his heart to win her and he takes on himself a full-time, all-engaging pursuit. Thereafter he will have room for little else. Thereafter his whole life will be filled with seekings and findings, self-repudiations, tough disciplines and daily dyings as he is being crucified unto the world and the world unto him.

Were this an unfallen world the path of truth would be a smooth and easy one. Had the nature of man not suffered a huge moral dislocation there would be no discord between the way of God and the way of man. I assume that in heaven the angels live through a thousand serene millenniums without feeling the slightest discord between their desires and the will of God. But not so among men on earth. Here the natural man receives not the things of the Spirit of God; the flesh lusts against the Spirit and the Spirit against the flesh, and these are contrary one to the other. In that contest there can be only one outcome. We must surrender and God must have His way. His glory and our eternal welfare require that it be so.

Another reason that our religion must interfere with our private lives is that we live in the world, the Bible name for human society. The regenerated man has been inwardly separated from society as Israel was separated from Egypt at the crossing of the Red Sea. The Christian is a man of heaven temporarily living on earth. Though in spirit divided from the race of fallen men he must yet in the flesh live among them. In many things he is like them, but in others he differs so radically from them that they cannot but see and resent it. From the days of Cain and Abel the man of earth has punished the man of heaven for being different. The long history of persecution and martyrdom confirms this.

But we must not get the impression that the Christian life is one continuous conflict, one unbroken irritating struggle against the world, the flesh and the devil. A thousand times no. The heart that learns to die with Christ soon knows the blessed experience of rising with Him, and all the world's persecutions cannot still the high note of holy joy that springs up in the soul that has become the dwelling place of the Holy Spirit.

26

Each His Own Cross

An earnest Christian woman sought help from Henry Suso concerning her spiritual life. She had been imposing rigid austerities upon herself in an effort to feel the sufferings that Christ had felt on the cross. Things weren't going so well with her and Suso knew why.

The old saint wrote his spiritual daughter and reminded her that our Lord had not said, "If any man will come after me, let him deny himself, and take up *my* cross, and follow me." He had said, "Let him . . . take up *his* cross." There is a difference of only one small pronoun; but that difference is vast and important.

Crosses are all alike, but no two are identical. Never before nor since has there been a cross-experience just like that endured by the Saviour. The whole dreadful work of dying which Christ suffered was something unique in the experience of mankind. It had to be so if the cross was to mean life for the world. The sin-bearing, the darkness, the rejection by the Father were agonies peculiar to the Person of the holy sacrifice. To claim any experience remotely like that of Christ would be more than an error; it would be sacrilege.

Every cross was and is an instrument of death, but no man could die on the cross of another; each man died on his own cross; hence Jesus said, "Let him . . . take up *his* cross, and follow me."

Now there is a real sense in which the cross of Christ embraces all crosses and the death of Christ encompasses all deaths. "If one died for all, then were all dead" . . . "I am crucified with Christ" . . . "The cross of our Lord Jesus Christ, by whom the world is crucified unto me, and I unto the world." This is in the judicial working of God in redemption. The Christian as a member of the body of Christ is crucified along with his divine Head. Before God every true believer is reckoned to have died when Christ died. All subsequent experience of personal crucifixion is based upon this identification with Christ on the cross.

But in the practical, everyday outworking of the believer's crucifixion his own cross is brought into play. "Let him . . . take up *his* cross." That is obviously not the cross of Christ. Rather it is the believer's own personal cross by means of which the cross of Christ is made effective in slaying his evil nature and setting him free from its power.

The believer's own cross is one he has assumed voluntarily. Therein lies the difference between his cross and the cross on which Roman convicts died. They went to the cross against their will; he, because he chooses to do so. No Roman officer ever pointed to a cross and said, "If any man will, let him." Only Christ said that, and by so saying He placed the whole matter in the hands of the Christian. He can refuse to take his cross, or he can stoop and take it up and start for the dark hill. The difference between great sainthood and spiritual mediocrity depends upon which choice he makes.

To go along with Christ step by step and point by point in identical suffering of Roman crucifixion is not possible for any of us, and certainly is not intended by our Lord. What He does intend is that each of us should count himself dead indeed with Christ, and then accept willingly whatever of self-denial, repentance, humility and humble sacrifice that may be found in the path of obedient daily living. That is *his* cross, and it is the only one the Lord has invited him to bear.

27

Religion Should Produce Action

The supreme purpose of the Christian religion is to make men like God in order that they may act like God. In Christ the verbs *to be* and *to do* follow each other in that order.

True religion leads to moral action. The only true Christian is the practicing Christian. Such a one is in very reality an incarnation of Christ as Christ is the incarnation of God; not in the same degree and fullness of perfection, for there is nothing in the moral universe equal to that awful mystery of godliness which joined God and man in eternal union in the person of the Man Christ Jesus; but as the fullness of the Godhead was and is in Christ, so Christ is in the nature of the one who believes in Him in the manner prescribed in the Scriptures.

God always acts like Himself wherever He may be and whatever He may be doing. When God became flesh and dwelt among us He did not cease to act as He had been acting from eternity. "He veiled His deity but He did not void it." The ancient flame dimmed down to spare the helpless eyes of mortal men, but as much as was seen was true fire. Christ restrained His powers but He did not violate His holiness. In whatsoever He did He was holy, harmless, separate from sinners and higher than the highest heaven.

Just as in eternity God acted like Himself and when incarnated in human flesh still continued in all His conduct to be true to His holiness, so does He when He enters the nature of a believing man. This is the method by which He makes the redeemed man holy. He enters a human nature at regeneration as He once entered human nature at the incarnation and acts as becomes God, using that nature as a medium of expression for His moral perfections.

Cicero, the Roman orator, once warned his hearers that they were in danger of making philosophy a substitute for action instead of allowing it to produce action. What is true of philosophy is true also of religion. The faith of Christ was never intended to be an end in itself nor to serve instead of something else. In the minds of some teachers faith stands in lieu of moral conduct and every inquirer after God must take his choice between the two. We are presented with the well-known either/or: either we have faith or we have works, and faith saves while works damn us. Hence the tremendous emphasis on faith and the apologetic, mincing approach to the doctrine of personal holiness in modern evangelism. This error has lowered the moral standards of the church and helped to lead us into the wilderness where we currently find ourselves.

Rightly understood, faith is not a substitute for moral conduct but a means toward it. The tree does not serve in lieu of fruit but as an agent by which fruit is secured. Fruit, not trees, is the end God has in mind in yonder orchard; so Christ-like conduct is the end of Christian faith. To oppose faith to works is to make the fruit the enemy to the tree; yet that is exactly what we have managed to do. And the consequences have been disastrous.

A miscalculation in laying the foundation of a building will throw the whole superstructure out of plumb, and the error that gave us faith as a substitute for action instead of faith in action has raised up in our day unsymmetrical and ugly temples of which we may well be ashamed and for which we shall surely give a strict account in the day when Christ judges the secrets of our hearts.

In practice we may detect the subtle (and often uncon-

scious) substitution when we hear a Christian assure
someone that he will "pray over" his problem, knowing
full well that he intends to use prayer as a substitute for
service. It is much easier to pray that a poor friend's needs
may be supplied than to supply them. James' words burn
with irony: "If a brother or sister be naked, and destitute of
daily food, and one of you say unto them, Depart in peace,
be ye warmed and filled; notwithstanding ye give them not
those things which are needful to the body; what doth it
profit?" And the mystical John sees also the incongruity
involved in substituting religion for action: "But whoso
hath this world's good, and seeth his brother have need,
and shutteth up his bowels of compassion from him, how
dwelleth the love of God in him? My little children, let us
not love in word, neither in tongue; but in deed and in
truth. And hereby we know that we are of the truth, and
shall assure our hearts before him."

A proper understanding of this whole thing will destroy
the false and artificial either/or. Then we will have not less
faith but more godly works; not less praying but more
serving; not fewer words but more holy deeds; not weaker
profession but more courageous possession; not a religion
as a substitute for action but religion in faith-filled action.

And what is that but to say that we will have come again
to the teaching of the New Testament?

Excerpts from
Man, The Dwelling Place of God

The Once-Born and the Twice-Born
The Communion of Saints
Does God Always Answer Prayer?
The Importance of Sound Doctrine

28

The Once-Born and the Twice-Born

Classification is one of the most difficult of all tasks. Even in the realm of religion there are enough lights and shades to make it injudicious to draw too fine a line between men and men. If the religious world were composed of squares of solid black and solid white classification would be easy; but unfortunately it is not.

It is a grave error for us evangelicals to assume that the children of God are all in our communion and that all who are not associated with us are *ipso facto* enemies of the Lord. The Pharisees made that mistake and crucified Christ as a consequence.

With all this in mind, and leaning over backwards to be fair and charitable, there is yet one distinction which we dare make, which indeed we *must* make if we are to think the thoughts of God after Him and bring our beliefs into harmony with the Holy Scriptures. That distinction is the one which exists between two classes of human beings, the once-born and the twice-born.

That such a distinction does in fact exist was taught by our Lord with great plainness of speech, in contexts which preclude the possibility that He was merely speaking figuratively. "Except man be born again, he cannot see the kingdom of God," He said, and the whole chapter where these words are found confirms that He was speaking precisely, setting forth meanings as blunt and downright as it is possible for language to convey.

"Ye must be born again," said Christ. "That which is born of the flesh is flesh; and that which is born of the Spirit is spirit." This clear line of demarcation runs through the entire New Testament, quite literally dividing one human being from another and making a distinction as sharp as that which exists between different genera of the animal kingdom.

Just who belongs to one class and who to the other it is not always possible to judge, though the two kinds of life ordinarily separate from each other. Those who are twice-born crystallize around the Person of Christ and cluster together in companies, while the once-born are held together only by the ties of nature, aided by the ties of race or by common political and social interests.

Our Lord warned His disciples that they would be persecuted. "In the world ye shall have tribulation," He said, and "Blessed are they which are persecuted for righteousness' sake: for theirs is the kingdom of heaven. Blessed are ye, when men shall revile you, and persecute you, and shall say all manner of evil against you falsely, for my sake."

These are only two of many passages of the New Testament warning of persecution or recording the fact of harassment and attack suffered by the followers of the Lord. This same idea runs through the entire Bible from the once-born Cain who slew the twice-born Abel to the Book of the Revelation where the end of human history comes in a burst of blood and fire.

That hostility exists between the once-born and the twice-born is known to every student of the Bible; the reason for it was stated by Christ when He said, "If ye were of the world, the world would love his own: but because ye are not of the world, but I have chosen you out of the world, therefore the world hateth you." The rule was laid down by the apostle Paul when he wrote, "But as then he that was born after the flesh persecuted him that was born after the Spirit, even so it is now."

Difference of moral standards between the once-born

and the twice-born, and their opposite ways of life, may be contributing causes of this hostility; but the real cause lies deeper. There are two spirits abroad in the earth: the spirit that works in the children of disobedience and the Spirit of God. These two can never be reconciled in time or in eternity. The spirit that dwells in the once-born is forever opposed to the Spirit that inhabits the heart of the twice-born. This hostility began somewhere in the remote past before the creation of man and continues to this day. The modern effort to bring peace between these two spirits is not only futile but contrary to the moral laws of the universe.

To teach that the spirit of the once-born is at enmity with the Spirit of the twice-born is to bring down upon one's head every kind of violent abuse. No language is too bitter to hurl against the conceited bigot who would dare to draw such a line of distinction between men. Such malignant ideas are at odds with the brotherhood of man, says the once-born, and are held only by the apostles of disunity and hate. This mighty rage against the twice-born only serves to confirm the truth they teach. But this no one seems to notice.

What we need to restore power to the Christian testimony is not soft talk about brotherhood but an honest recognition that two human races occupy the earth simultaneously: a fallen race that sprang from the loins of Adam and a regenerate race that is born of the Spirit through the redemption which is in Christ Jesus.

To accept this truth requires a tough-mindedness and a spiritual maturity that modern Christians simply do not possess. To face up to it hardly contributes to that "peace of mind" after which our religious weaklings bleat so plaintively.

For myself, I long ago decided that I would rather know the truth than be happy in ignorance. If I cannot have both truth and happiness, give me truth. We'll have a long time to be happy in heaven.

29

The Communion of Saints

I believe in the communion of saints.
Apostles' Creed

These words were written into the creed about the middle of the fifth century.

It would be difficult if not altogether impossible for us at this late date to know exactly what was in the minds of the Church Fathers who introduced the words into the creed, but in the Book of Acts we have a description of the first Christian communion: "Then they that gladly received his word were baptized: and the same day there were added unto them about three thousand souls. And they continued stedfastly in the apostles' doctrine and fellowship, and in breaking of bread, and in prayers."

Here is the original apostolic fellowship, the pattern after which every true Christian communion must be modeled.

The word "fellowship," in spite of its abuses, is still a beautiful and meaningful word. When rightly understood it means the same as the word "communion," that is, the act and condition of sharing together in some common blessing by numbers of persons. The communion of saints, then, means an intimate and loving sharing together of certain spiritual blessings by persons who are on an equal

From *Foundations of the Faith*, Fleming H. Revell, Westwood, N.J. Used by permission.

footing before the blessing in which they share. This fellowship must include every member of the Church of God from Pentecost to this present moment and on to the end of the age.

Now, before there can be *communion* there must be *union*. The sharers are one in a sense altogether above organization, nationality, race or denomination. That oneness is a divine thing, achieved by the Holy Spirit in the act of regeneration. Whoever is born of God is one with everyone else who is born of God. Just as gold is always gold, wherever and in whatever shape it is found, and every detached scrap of gold belongs to the true family and is composed of the same elements, so every regenerate soul belongs to the universal Christian community and to the fellowship of the saints.

Every redeemed soul is born out of the same spiritual life as every other redeemed soul and partakes of the divine nature in exactly the same manner. Each one is thus made a member of the Christian community and a sharer in everything which that community enjoys. This is the true communion of saints. But to know this is not enough. If we would enter into the power of it we must exercise ourselves in this truth; we must *practice* thinking and praying with the thought that we are members of the Body of Christ and brothers to all the ransomed saints living and dead who have believed on Christ and acknowledged Him as Lord.

We have said that the communion of saints is a fellowship, a sharing in certain divinely given things by divinely called persons. Now, what are those things?

The first and most important is *life*—"the life of God in the soul of man," to borrow a phrase from Henry Scougal. This life is the basis of everything else which is given and shared. And that life is nothing else than God Himself. It should be evident that there can be no true Christian sharing unless there is first an impartation of life. An organization and a name do not make a church. One hundred religious persons knit into a unity by careful organization do not constitute a church any more than eleven dead men make a football team. The first requisite is life, always.

The apostolic fellowship is also a fellowship of *truth*. The inclusiveness of the fellowship must always be held along with the exclusiveness of it. Truth brings into its gracious circle all who admit and accept the Bible as the source of all truth and the Son of God as the Saviour of men. But there dare be no weak compromise with the facts, no sentimental mouthing of the old phrases: "We are all headed for the same place.... Each one is seeking in his own way to please the Father and make heaven his home." The truth makes men free, and the truth will bind and loose, will open and shut, will include and exclude at its high will without respect to persons. To reject or deny the truth of the Word is to exclude ourselves from the apostolic communion.

Now, someone may ask, "What is the truth of which you speak? Is my fate to depend upon Baptist truth or Presbyterian truth or Anglican truth, or all of these or none of these? To know the communion of saints must I believe in Calvinism or Arminianism? In the Congregational or the Episcopal form of church government? Must I interpret prophecy in accord with the premillenarians or the post-millenarians? Must I believe in immersion or sprinkling or pouring?" The answer to all this is easy. The confusion is only apparent, not actual.

The early Christians, under the fire of persecution, driven from place to place, sometimes deprived of the opportunity for careful instruction in the faith, wanted a "rule" which would sum up all that they must believe to assure their everlasting welfare. Out of this critical need arose the creeds. Of the many, the Apostles' Creed is the best known and best loved, and has been reverently repeated by the largest number of believers through the centuries. And for millions of good men that creed contains the essentials of truth. Not all truths, to be sure, but the heart of all truth. It served in trying days as a kind of secret password that instantly united men to each other when passed from lip to lip by the followers of the Lamb. It is fair to say, then, that the truth shared by saints in the apostolic fellowship is the same truth which is outlined for convenience in the Apostles' Creed.

In this day when the truth of Christianity is under serious fire from so many directions it is most important that we know what we believe and that we guard it carefully. But in our effort to interpret and expound the Holy Scriptures in accord with the ancient faith of all Christians, we should remember that a seeking soul may find salvation through the blood of Christ while yet knowing little of the fuller teachings of Christian theology. We must, therefore, admit to our fellowship every sheep who has heard the voice of the Shepherd and has tried to follow Him.

The beginner in Christ who has not yet had time to learn much Christian truth and the underprivileged believer who has had the misfortune to be brought up in a church where the Word has been neglected from the pulpit, are very much in the same situation. Their faith grasps only a small portion of truth, and their "sharing" is necessarily limited to the small portion they grasp. The important thing, however, is that the little bit they do enjoy is *real truth*. It may be no more than this, that "Christ Jesus came into the world to save sinners"; but if they walk in the light of that much truth, no more is required to bring them into the circle of the blessed and to constitute them true members of the apostolic fellowship.

Then, true Christian communion consists in the sharing of a *Presence*. This is not poetry merely, but a fact taught in bold letters in the New Testament. God has given us Himself in the Person of His Son. "Where two or three are gathered together in my name, there am I in the midst of them." The immanence of God in His universe makes possible the enjoyment of the "real Presence" by the saints of God in heaven and on earth simultaneously. Wherever they may be, He is present to them in the fullness of His Godhead.

I do not believe that the Bible teaches the possibility of communication between the saints on earth and those in heaven. But while there cannot be communication, there most surely can be communion. Death does not tear the individual believer from his place in the Body of Christ. As in our human bodies each member is nourished by the same blood which at once gives life and unity to the entire organism, so in the Body of Christ the quickening Spirit flowing through every part gives life and unity to the whole. Our Christian brethren who have gone from our sight retain still their place in the universal fellowship. The Church is one, whether waking or sleeping, by a unity of life forevermore.

The most important thing about the doctrine of the communion of saints is its practical effects on the lives of Christians. We know very little about the saints above, but about the saints on earth we know, or can know, a great deal. We Protestants do not believe (since the Bible does not teach) that the saints who have gone into heaven before us are in any way affected by the prayers or labors of saints who remain on earth. Our particular care is not for those whom God has already honored with the vision beatific, but for the hard-pressed and strugggling pilgrims who are still traveling toward the City of God. We all belong to each other; the spiritual welfare of each one is or should be the loving concern of all the rest.

We should pray for an enlargement of soul to receive into our hearts all of God's people, whatever their race, color or church affiliation. Then we should practice thinking of ourselves as members of the blessed family of God and should strive in prayer to love and appreciate everyone who is born of the Father.

I suggest also that we try to acquaint ourselves as far as possible with the good and saintly souls who lived before our times and now belong to the company of the redeemed in heaven. How sad to limit our sympathies to those of our own day, when God in His providence has made it possible for us to enjoy the rich treasures of the minds and hearts of so many holy and gifted saints of other days. To confine our reading to the works of a few favorite authors of today or last week is to restrict our horizons and to pinch our souls dangerously.

I have no doubt that the prayerful reading of some of the great spiritual classics of the centuries would destroy in us forever that constriction of soul which seems to be the earmark of modern evangelicalism.

For many of us the wells of the past wait to be reopened. Augustine, for instance, would bring to us a sense of the overwhelming majesty of God that would go far to cure the flippancy of spirit found so widely among modern Christians. Bernard of Cluny would sing to us of "Jerusalem the Golden" and the peace of an eternal sabbath day until the miserable pleasures of this world become intolerable; Richard Rolle would show us how to escape from "the abundance of riches, the flattering of women and the fairness of youth," that we may go on to know God with an intimacy that will become in our hearts "heat, fragrance and song"; Tersteegen would whisper to us of the "hidden love of God" and the awful Presence until our hearts would become "still before Him" and "prostrate inwardly adore Him"; before our eyes the sweet St. Francis would throw his arms of love around sun and moon, trees and rain, bird and beast, and thank God for them all in a pure rapture of spiritual devotion.

But who is able to complete the roster of the saints? To them we owe a debt of gratitude too great to comprehend: prophet and apostle, martyr and reformer, scholar and translator, hymnist and composer, teacher and evangelist, not to mention ten thousand times ten thousand simplehearted and anonymous souls who kept the flame of pure religion alive even in those times when the faith of our fathers was burning but dimly all over the world.

They belong to us, all of them, and we belong to them. They and we and all redeemed men and women of whatever age or clime are included in the universal fellowship of Christ, and together compose "a royal priesthood, an holy nation, a peculiar people," who enjoy a common but blessed communion of saints.

30

Does God Always Answer Prayer?

Contrary to popular opinion, the cultivation of a psychology of uncritical belief is not an unqualified good, and if carried too far it may be a positive evil. The whole world has been booby-trapped by the devil, and the deadliest trap of all is the religious one. Error never looks so innocent as when it is found in the sanctuary.

One field where harmless-looking but deadly traps appear in great profusion is the field of prayer. There are more sweet notions about prayer than could be contained in a large book, all of them wrong and all highly injurious to the souls of men.

I think of one such false notion that is found often in pleasant places consorting smilingly with other notions of unquestionable orthodoxy. It is that *God always answers prayer.*

This error appears among the saints as a kind of all-purpose philosophic therapy to prevent any disappointed Christian from suffering too great a shock when it becomes evident to him that his prayer expectations are not being fulfilled. It is explained that God always answers prayer, either by saying Yes or by saying No, or by substituting something else for the desired favor.

Now, it would be hard to invent a neater trick than this to save face for the petitioner whose requests have been rejected for nonobedience. Thus when a prayer is not answered he has but to smile brightly and explain, "God said No." It is all so very comfortable. His wobbly faith is saved from confusion and his conscience is permitted to lie undisturbed. But I wonder if it is honest.

To receive an answer to prayer as the Bible uses the term and as Christians have understood it historically, two elements must be present: (1) A clear-cut request made to God for a specific favor. (2) A clear-cut granting of that favor by God in answer to the request. There must be no semantic twisting, no changing of labels, no altering of the map during the journey to help the embarrassed tourist to find himself.

When we go to God with a request that He modify the existing situation for us, that is, that He answer prayer, there are two conditions that we must meet: (1) We must pray in the will of God and (2) we must be on what old-fashioned Christians often call "praying ground"; that is, we must be living lives pleasing to God.

It is futile to beg God to act contrary to His revealed purposes. To pray with confidence the petitioner must be certain that his request falls within the broad will of God for His people.

The second condition is also vitally important. God has not placed Himself under obligation to honor the requests of worldly, carnal or disobedient Christians. He hears and answers the prayers only of those who walk in His way. "Beloved, if our heart condemn us not, then have we confidence toward God. And whatsoever we ask, we receive of him, because we keep his commandments, and do those things that are pleasing in his sight .... If ye abide in me, and my words abide in you, ye shall ask what ye will, and it shall be done unto you" (I John 3:21, 22; John 15:7).

God wants us to pray and He wants to answer our prayers, but He makes our use of prayer as a privilege to commingle with His use of prayer as a discipline. To receive answers to prayer we must meet God's terms. If we neglect His commandments our petitions will not be honored. He will alter situations only at the request of obedient and humble souls.

The God-always-answers-prayer sophistry leaves the praying man without discipline. By the exercise of this bit of smooth casuistry he ignores the necessity to live soberly, righteously and godly in this present world, and actually takes God's flat refusal to answer his prayer as the very answer itself. Of course such a man will not grow in holiness; he will never learn how to wrestle and wait; he will never know correction; he will not hear the voice of God calling him forward; he will never arrive at the place where he is morally and spiritually fit to have his prayers answered. His wrong philosophy has ruined him.

That is why I turn aside to expose the bit of bad theology upon which his bad philosophy is founded. The man who accepts it never knows where he stands; he never knows whether or not he has true faith, for if his request is not granted he avoids the implication by the simple dodge of declaring that God switched the whole thing around and gave him something else. He will not allow himself to shoot at a target, so he cannot tell how good or how bad a marksman he is.

Of certain persons James says plainly: "Ye ask, and receive not, because ye ask amiss, that ye may consume it upon your lusts." From that brief sentence we may learn that God refuses some requests because they who make them are not morally worthy to receive the answer. But this means nothing to the one who has been seduced into the belief that God always answers prayer. When such a man asks and receives not he passes his hand over the hat and comes up with the answer in some other form. One thing he clings to with great tenacity: God never turns anyone away, but invariably grants every request.

The truth is that God always answers the prayer that accords with His will as revealed in the Scriptures, provided the one who prays is obedient and trustful. Further than this we dare not go.

31

The Importance of Sound Doctrine

It would be impossible to overemphasize the importance of sound doctrine in the life of a Christian. Right thinking about all spiritual matters is imperative if we would have right living. As men do not gather grapes of thorns nor figs of thistles, so sound character does not grow out of unsound teaching.

The word *doctrine* means simply religious beliefs held and taught. It is the sacred task of all Christians, first as believers and then as teachers of religious beliefs, to be certain that these beliefs correspond exactly to truth. A precise agreement between belief and fact constitutes soundness in doctrine. We cannot afford to have less.

The apostles not only taught truth but contended for its purity against any who would corrupt it. The Pauline epistles resist every effort of false teachers to introduce doctrinal vagaries. John's epistles are sharp with condemnation of those teachers who harassed the young church by denying the incarnation and throwing doubts upon the doctrine of the Trinity; and Jude in his brief but powerful epistle rises to heights of burning eloquence as he pours scorn upon evil teachers who would mislead the saints.

Each generation of Christians must look to its beliefs. While truth itself is unchanging, the minds of men are porous vessels out of which truth can leak and into which error may seep to dilute the truth they contain. The human heart is heretical by nature and runs to error as naturally as a garden to weeds. All a man, a church or a denomination needs to guarantee deterioration of doctrine is to take everything for granted and do nothing. The unattended garden will soon be overrun with weeds; the heart that fails to cultivate truth and root out error will shortly be a theological wilderness; the church or denomination that grows careless on the highway of truth will before long find itself astray, bogged down in some mud flat from which there is no escape.

In every field of human thought and activity accuracy is considered a virtue. To err ever so slightly is to invite serious loss, if not death itself. Only in religious thought is faithfulness to truth looked upon as a fault. When men deal with things earthly and temporal they demand truth; when they come to the consideration of things heavenly and eternal they hedge and hesitate as if truth either could not be discovered or didn't matter anyway.

Montaigne said that a liar is one who is brave toward God and a coward toward men; for a liar faces God and shrinks from men. Is this not simply a proof of unbelief? Is it not to say that the liar believes in men but is not convinced of the existence of God, and is willing to risk the displeasure of a God who may not exist rather than that of man who obviously does?

I think also that deep, basic unbelief is back of human carelessness in religion. The scientist, the physician, the navigator deals with matters he knows are real; and because these things are real the world demands that both teacher and practitioner be skilled in the knowledge of them. The teacher of spiritual things only is required to be unsure in his beliefs, ambiguous in his remarks and tolerant of every religious opinion expressed by anyone, even by the man least qualified to hold an opinion.

Haziness of doctrine has always been the mark of the liberal. When the Holy Scriptures are rejected as the final authority on religious belief something must be found to take their place. Historically that something has been either reason or sentiment: if sentiment, it has been humanism. Sometimes there has been an admixture of the two, as may be seen in liberal churches today. These will not quite give up the Bible, neither will they quite believe it; the result is an unclear body of beliefs more like a fog than a mountain, where anything *may* be true but nothing may be trusted as being *certainly* true.

We have gotten accustomed to the blurred puffs of gray fog that pass for doctrine in modernistic churches and expect nothing better, but it is a cause for real alarm that the fog has begun of late to creep into many evangelical churches. From some previously unimpeachable sources are now coming vague statements consisting of a milky admixture of Scripture, science and human sentiment that is true to none of its ingredients because each one works to cancel the others out.

Certain of our evangelical brethren appear to be laboring under the impression that they are advanced thinkers because they are rethinking evolution and re-evaluating various Bible doctrines or even divine inspiration itself; but so far are they from being advanced thinkers that they are merely timid followers of modernism—fifty years behind the parade.

Little by little evangelical Christians these days are being brainwashed. One evidence is that increasing numbers of them are becoming ashamed to be found unequivocally on the side of truth. They say they believe but their beliefs have been so diluted as to be impossible of clear definition.

Moral power has always accompanied definitive beliefs. Great saints have always been dogmatic. We need right now a return to a gentle dogmatism that smiles while it stands stubborn and firm on the Word of God that liveth and abideth forever.

32

I Call It Heresy

As obedient children, not fashioning yourselves according to the former lusts in your ignorance.

I Peter 1:14

The scriptures do not teach that the Person of Jesus Christ nor any of the important offices which God has given Him can be divided or ignored according to the whims of men.

Therefore, I must be frank in my feeling that a notable heresy has come into being throughout our evangelical Christian circles—the widely-accepted concept that we humans can choose to accept Christ only because we need Him as Saviour and that we have the right to postpone our obedience to Him as Lord as long as we want to!

This concept has sprung naturally from a misunderstanding of what the Bible actually says about Christian discipleship and obedience. It is now found in nearly all of our full gospel literature. I confess that I was among those who preached it before I began to pray earnestly, to study diligently and meditate with anguish over the whole matter.

I think the following is a fair statement of what I was taught in my early Christian experience and it certainly needs a lot of modifying and a great many qualifiers to save us from being in error:

"We are saved by accepting Christ as our Saviour;
We are sanctified by accepting Christ as our Lord;
We may do the first without doing the second!"

The truth is that salvation apart from obedience is unknown in the sacred scriptures. Peter makes it plain that we are "elect according to the foreknowledge of God the Father, through sanctification of the Spirit unto obedience."

What a tragedy that in our day we often hear the gospel appeal made on this kind of basis:

"Come to Jesus! You do not have to obey anyone. You do not have to change anything. You do not have to give up anything, alter anything, surrender anything, give back anything—just come to Him and believe in Him as Saviour!"

So they come and believe in the Saviour. Later on, in a meeting or conference, they will hear another appeal:

"Now that you have received Him as Saviour, how would you like to take Him as Lord?"

The fact that we hear this everywhere does not make it right. To urge men and women to believe in a divided Christ is bad teaching for no one can receive half of Christ, or a third of Christ, or a quarter of the Person of Christ! We are not saved by believing in an office nor in a work.

I have heard well-meaning workers say, "Come and believe on the finished work." That work will not save you. The Bible does not tell us to believe in an office or a work, but to believe on the Lord Jesus Christ Himself, the Person who has done that work and holds those offices.

Now, note again, Peter's emphasis on obedience among the scattered and persecuted Christians of his day.

It seems most important to me that Peter speaks of his fellow Christians as "obedient children." He was not giving them a command or an exhortation to be obedient. In effect, he said, "Assuming that you are believers, I therefore gather that you are also obedient. So now, as obedient children, do so and so."

Brethren, I would point out that obedience is taught throughout the entire Bible and that true obedience is one of the toughest requirements of the Christian life. Apart from obedience, there can be no salvation, for salvation without obedience is a self-contradictory impossibility.

The essence of sin is rebellion against divine authority.

God said to Adam and Eve, "Thou shalt not eat from this tree, and in the day that thou eatest thereof thou shalt surely die." Here was a divine requirement calling for obedience on the part of those who had the power of choice and will.

In spite of the strong prohibition, Adam and Eve stretched forth their hands and tasted of the fruit and thus they disobeyed and rebelled, bringing sin upon themselves.

Paul writes very plainly and directly in the Book of Romans about "one man's disobedience"—and this is a stern word by the Holy Spirit through the Apostle—by one man's disobedience came the downfall of the human race!

In John's Gospel, the Word is very plain and clear that sin is lawlessness, that sin is disobedience to the law of God. Paul's picture of sinners in Ephesians concludes that "the people of the world are the children of disobedience." Paul certainly means that disobedience characterizes them, conditions them, molds them. Disobedience has become a part of their nature.

All of this provides background for the great, continuing question before the human race: "Who is boss?" This breaks down into a series of three questions: "To whom do I belong?" "To whom do I owe allegiance?" and "Who has authority to require obedience of me?"

Now, I suppose of all the people in the world Americans have the most difficult time in giving obedience to anyone or anything. Americans are supposed to be sons of freedom. We ourselves were the outcropping of a revolt. We spawned a revolution, pouring the tea overboard in Boston harbor. We made speeches and said, "The sound of the clash of arms is carried on every wind that blows from the Boston Commons" and finally, "Give me liberty or give me death!"

That is in the American blood and when anyone says, "You owe obedience," we immediately bristle! In the natural sense, we do not take kindly to the prospect of yielding obedience to anyone.

In the same sense, the people of this world have a quick and ready answer to the questions: "To whom do I belong?" and "To whom do I owe obedience?"

Their answer is: "I belong to myself. No one has authority to require my obedience!"

Our generation makes a great deal out of this, and we give it the name of "individualism." On the basis of our individuality we claim the right of self-determination.

In an airplane, the pilot who sits at the controls determines where that plane is going. He must determine the destination.

Now, if God had made us humans to be mere machines we would not have the power of self-determination. But since He made us in His own image and made us to be moral creatures, He has given us that power of self-determination.

I would insist that we do not have the right of self-determination because God has given us only the power to choose evil. Seeing that God is a holy God and we are moral creatures having the power but not the right to choose evil, no man has any right to lie.

We have the power to lie but no man has any right to lie.

We have the power to steal—I could go out and get myself a better coat than the one I own. I could slip out through a side door and get away with the coat. I have that power but I do not have that right!

I have the power to use a knife, a razor or a gun to kill another person—but I do not have that right! I have only the power to do it.

Actually, we only have the right to be good—we never

have the right to be bad because God is good. We only have the right to be holy; we never have the right to be unholy. If you are unholy you are using a right that is not yours. Adam and Eve had no moral right to eat of that tree of good and evil, but they took it and usurped the right that was not theirs.

The poet Tennyson must have thought about this for he wrote in his *In Memoriam:* "Our wills are ours, we know not how; our wills are ours to make them Thine!"

Oh, this mystery of man's free will is far too great for us! Tennyson said, "We know not how." But then he girds himself and continues, "Yes, our wills are ours to make them Thine." And that is the only right we have here to make our wills the wills of God, to make the will of God our will!

We must remember that God is Who He is and we are what we are. God is the Sovereign and we are the creatures. He is the Creator and therefore He has a right to command us with the obligation that we should obey. It is a happy obligation, I might say, for "His yoke is easy and His burden is light."

Now, this is where I raise the point again of our human insistence that Christ may sustain a divided relationship toward us. This is now so commonly preached that to oppose it or object to it means that you are sticking your neck out and you had best be prepared for what comes.

But how can we insist and teach that our Lord Jesus Christ can be our Saviour without being our Lord? How can we continue to teach that we can be saved without any thought of obedience to our Sovereign Lord?

I am satisfied that when a man believes on Jesus Christ he must believe on the whole Lord Jesus Christ—not making any reservation! I am satisfied that it is wrong to look upon Jesus as a kind of divine nurse to whom we can go when sin has made us sick, and after He has helped us, to say "Goodbye"—and go on our own way.

Suppose I slip into a hospital and tell the staff, I need a

blood transfusion or perhaps an X-ray of my gall bladder. After they have ministered to me and given their services, do I just slip out of the hospital again with a cheery "Goodbye"—as though I owe them nothing and it was kind of them to help me in my time of need?

That may sound like a grotesque concept to you, but it does pretty well draw the picture of those who have been taught that they can use Jesus as a Saviour in their time of need without owning Him as Sovereign and Lord and without owing Him obedience and allegiance.

The Bible never in any way gives us such a concept of salvation. Nowhere are we ever led to believe that we can use Jesus as a Saviour and not own Him as our Lord. He is the Lord and as the Lord He saves us, because He has all of the offices of Saviour and Christ and High Priest and Wisdom and Righteousness and Sanctification and Redemption! He is all of these things and all of these are embodied in Him as Christ the Lord.

My brethren, we are not allowed to come to Jesus Christ as shrewd, clever operators saying, "We will take this and this, but we won't take that!" We do not come to Him as one who, buying furniture for his house, declares: "I will take this table but I don't want that chair"—dividing it up!

No, sir! It is either all of Christ or none of Christ!

I believe we need to preach again a whole Christ to the world—a Christ who does not need our apologies, a Christ who will not be divided, a Christ who will either be Lord of all or who will not be Lord at all!

I think it is important to agree that true salvation restores the right of a Creator-creature relationship because it acknowledges God's right to our fellowship and communion.

You see, in our time we have over-emphasized the psychology of the sinner's condition. We spend much time describing the woe of the sinner, the grief of the sinner, and the great burden he carries. He does have all of these, but we have over-emphasized them until we forget the principal fact—that the sinner is actually a rebel against properly-constituted authority!

That is what makes sin, sin. We are rebels. We are sons of disobedience. Sin is the breaking of the law and we are in rebellion and we are fugitives from the just laws of God while we are sinners.

By way of illustration, suppose a man escapes from prison. Certainly he will have grief. He is going to be in pain after bumping logs and stones and fences as he crawls and hides away in the dark. He is going to be hungry and cold and weary. His beard will grow long and he will be tired and cramped and cold—all of these will happen, but they are incidental to the fact that he is a fugitive from justice and a rebel against law.

So it is with sinners. Certainly they are heartbroken and they carry a heavy load. Certainly they labor and are heavy-laden. The Bible takes full account of these things; but they are incidental to the fact that the reason the sinner is what he is, is because he has rebelled against the laws of God and he is a fugitive from divine judgment.

It is that which constitutes the nature of sin; not the fact that he carries a heavy load of misery and sadness and guilt. These things constitute only the outcropping of the sinful nature, but the root of sin is rebellion against law, rebellion against God. Does not the sinner say: "I belong to myself—I owe allegiance to no one unless I choose to give it!" That is the essence of sin.

But thankfully, salvation reverses that and restores the former relationship so that the first thing the returning sinner does is to confess: "Father, I have sinned against heaven and in Thy sight, and I am no more worthy to be called Thy son. Make me as one of Thy hired servants."

Thus, in repentance, we reverse that relationship and we fully submit to the Word of God and the will of God, as obedient children.

Now the happiness of all the moral creatures lies right here, brethren, in the giving of obedience to God. The

Psalmist cried out in Psalm 103: "Bless the Lord, ye his angels, that excel in strength, that do his commandments, hearkening unto the voice of his word."

The angels in heaven find their complete freedom and highest happiness in obeying the commandments of God. They do not find it a tyranny—they find it a delight.

I have been looking again into the mysteries in the first chapter of Ezekiel and I don't understand it. There are creatures with four faces and four wings, strange beings doing strange things. They have wheels and still other wheels in the middle of the wheels. There is fire coming out of the north and there are creatures going straight ahead and some that lower their wings and wave them. Strange, beautiful beings and they are all having the time of their lives. Utterly, completely delighted with the Presence of God and that they could serve God!

Heaven is a place of surrender to the whole will of God and it is heaven because it is such a place.

On the other hand, hell is certainly the world of disobedience. Everything else that may be said about hell may be true, but this one thing is the essence—hell is the world of the rebel! Hell is the Alcatraz for the unconstituted rebels who refuse to surrender to the will of God.

I thank God that heaven is the world of God's obedient children. Whatever else we may say of its pearly gates, its golden streets and its jasper walls, heaven is heaven because it is the world of obedient children. Heaven is heaven because children of the Most High God find they are in their normal sphere as obedient moral beings.

Jesus said there are fire and worms in hell, but that is not the reason it is hell. You might endure worms and fire, but for a moral creature to know and realize that he is where he is because he is a rebel—that is the essence of hell and judgment. It is the eternal world of all the disobedient rebels who have said, "I owe God nothing!"

This is the time given us to decide. Each person makes his own decision as to the eternal world he is going to inhabit.

This is a serious matter of decision. You do not come to this decision as though it were a matter of being interviewed for a job or getting your diploma at a school.

We have no basis to believe that we can come casually and sprightly to the Lord Jesus and say, "I have come for some help, Lord Jesus. I understand that you are the Saviour so I am going to believe and be saved and then I am going to turn away and think about the other matters of lordship and allegiance and obedience at some time in the future."

I warn you—you will not get help from Him in that way for the Lord will not save those whom He cannot command!

He will not divide His offices. You cannot believe on a half-Christ. We take Him for what He is—the anointed Saviour and Lord who is King of kings and Lord of all lords! He would not be Who He is if He saved us and called us and chose us without the understanding that He can also guide and control our lives.

Brethren, I believe in the deeper Christian life and experience—oh yes! But I believe we are mistaken when we try to add the deeper life to an imperfect salvation, obtained imperfectly by an imperfect concept of the whole thing.

Under the working of the Spirit of God through such men as Finney and Wesley, no one would ever dare to rise in a meeting and say, "I am a Christian" if he had not surrendered his whole being to God and had taken Jesus Christ as his Lord as well as his Saviour, and had brought himself under obedience to the will of the Lord. It was only then that he could say, "I am saved!"

Today, we let them say they are saved no matter how imperfect and incomplete the transaction, with the proviso that the deeper Christian life can be tacked on at some time in the future.

Can it be that we really think that we do not owe Jesus Christ our obedience?

We have owed Him our obedience ever since the second

we cried out to Him for salvation, and if we do not give Him that obedience, I have reason to wonder if we are really converted!

I see things and I hear of things that Christian people are doing and as I watch them operate within the profession of Christianity I do raise the question of whether they have been truly converted.

Brethren, I believe it is the result of faulty teaching to begin with. They thought of the Lord as a hospital and Jesus as chief of staff to fix up poor sinners that had gotten into trouble!

"Fix me up, Lord," they have insisted, "so that I can go on my own way!"

That is bad teaching, brethren. It is filled with self-deception. Let us look unto Jesus our Lord, high, holy, wearing the crowns, Lord of lords and King of all, having a perfect right to command full obedience from all of His saved people!

Just remember what the Bible says about the Person and the titles and the offices of Jesus:

"God hath made this same Jesus whom ye have crucified both Lord and Christ." Jesus means Saviour, Lord means Sovereign, Christ means Anointed One. The Apostle, therefore, did not preach Jesus as Saviour—he preached to them Jesus as Lord and Christ and Saviour, never dividing His person or offices.

Remember, too, that Paul wrote to the Roman Christians:

"What saith it? The word is nigh thee, even in thy mouth, and in thy heart: that is, the word of faith, which we preach; that if thou shalt confess with thy mouth the Lord Jesus, and shalt believe in thine heart that God hath raised him from the dead, thou shalt be saved."

The Apostle did not say that "Thou shalt confess with thy mouth the Saviour." He said, "Thou shalt confess with thy mouth the Lord Jesus, for with the heart man believeth unto righteousness; and with the mouth confession is made unto salvation; . . . for there is no difference between Jew and Greek: for the same Lord over all is rich unto all that call upon him. For whosoever shall call upon the name of the Lord shall be saved."

Three times he calls Jesus Lord in these passages telling us how to be saved. He says that faith in the Lord Jesus plus confession of that faith to the world brings salvation to us!

God desires that we be honest with Him above everything else. Search the scriptures, read the New Testament, and if you see that I have given a germ of truth, then I urge you to do something about it. If you have been led to believe imperfectly in a divided Saviour, be glad that there is still time for you to do something about it!

33

The Bible Is Not Dated

... the word of God, which liveth and abideth for ever....
And this is the word which by the gospel is preached unto you.

I Peter 1:23, 25

There are Christians among us today who seem to feel that their spiritual lives would have been greatly helped if they could have had voice-to-voice and person-to-person counsel from our Lord or from the Apostle Peter or Paul.

I know it is fair to say that if one of the apostles or any of the great early fathers of the church could return to this world from their yesteryear, there would not be room to contain the crowds that would rush in.

If it were known that St. Augustine or Chrysostom or Francis of Assissi or Knox or Luther or any of the great who have lived were to be present to speak, we would all give our closest attention and listen as though we were hearing indeed a very word from God.

Under the circumstances, we cannot hope to hear from men of God who centuries ago completed their ministries and went to be with the Lord. The voices of the great saints and mighty warriors of yesterday can no longer be heard in this twentieth century.

However, there is good news for those who are anxious to hear a word from the Lord! If we have a mind to listen, we may still "hear" the voice of an apostle for we are dealing with the words written by the man, Peter. He was indeed a great saint, even though we may not consider him the greatest of the apostles. I think it is safe to say that he was the second of the apostles. Paul alone, perhaps, having a higher place than the man, Peter.

So, as we look into his message, Peter will be speaking to us, even though it is through an "interpreter."

Often our missionaries have told us of difficult times they have had with interpreters. The expression of the missionary may go in one way and come out with a different sense to the hearer, and I think when we expound the scriptures, we are often guilty of being imperfect interpreters. I shall do the best I can to catch the spirit of the man, Peter, and to determine what God is trying to say to us and to reduce the interference to a minimum.

Now, I suppose more people would like me if I were to declare that I preach the Bible and nothing but the Bible. I attempt to do that, but honesty compels me to say that the best I can do is to preach the Bible as I understand it. I trust that through your prayers and the Spirit of Christ my understanding may be right. If you pray and if I yield and trust, perhaps what we get from First Peter will indeed be approximately what Peter would say if he were here in person. We will stay as close as we can to the Word of the Living God.

The man Peter had a reputation for being first because he was a most impetuous man. He was either the first or among the very first in almost everything that took place and that touched him while he was alive.

For this reason, I suppose that Peter would have made a wonderful American! He usually opened his mouth and talked before he thought and that is a characteristic of many of us. He rushed to do what he had to do—and that is also characteristic of us.

From the record of the Gospels, it appears that Peter may have been the first, or at least among the very first, to become a disciple of John the Baptist. He was among the first disciples who turned to Jesus when John the Baptist pointed and said, "Behold the Lamb of God that taketh away the sins of the world."

Peter was the first apostle called by our Lord to follow Him. I believe that Peter was the first convert for he was the first man to say, "Thou art the Son of the Living God."

Peter was among the very first to see our Lord after He had risen from the dead. There are those who insist that Peter was the first, believing that the Lord Jesus appeared to no one else until after a meeting with His beloved friend, Peter.

Also, remember that Peter was the first of the New Testament preachers. It is quite in keeping with the temperament of this man that when the Holy Spirit had come at Pentecost and there was opportunity for someone to stand and speak the Truth, Peter should be the man to do it.

I think there is no profound theological reason back of this. I think it is a matter of temperament and disposition. When 120 persons are suddenly filled with the Holy Spirit and it falls to the lot of one of them to leap up and express the wonder of what has just happened, it would be normal for the man Peter to be the one. So, he got to his feet and poured out that great sermon recorded in the second chapter of the Book of Acts—the great sermon that converted 3,000 persons!

But Peter was a man, and in his early discipleship and ministry there were glaring contradictions and inconsistencies in his life. It is not possible for us to try to boast and say that this man, this second greatest of the apostles, never deviated one inch from the straight line from the moment of his conversion to the time of his death. I do believe in realism in religion and I do not think any good can come from hiding the bad and trying to reflect an unnatural righteousness which is not true to the whole character of the man.

Actually, I wish that every one of us could be like the

angels or those strange creatures in the first chapter of Ezekiel, of whom it is said that when they went "they went every one straight forward."

I do not know what that means precisely, but I do know that it is an intriguing test—when they went they went straight forward. I wish that from the time I was converted at the age of 17 I had gone straight forward; but I did not and most of us have not. We zig-zag on our way to heaven in place of flying a straight course. I am sorry about this. I don't excuse it, but I try to understand it!

Well, Peter was a bundle of contradictions and I take the position that it further glorifies the grace of God that He could take a weak and vacillating and inconsistent man like Peter and make Saint Peter out of him!

Read again all that the New Testament says about Peter and you will find glaring contradictions. In His very first meeting with Peter, Jesus said, "Thou art Simon the son of Jona: thou shalt be called Cephas, which is by interpretation, A stone." Jesus Himself in calling Peter gave him this new name meaning a rock, which is of course a solid and unshaking thing.

But this man—this "rock"—was so wavering that he denied his Lord! He clipped off a man's ear in an impetuous act to defend his Master, yet within a few hours denied that he had ever met Jesus. He was prone to rush into a situation, to act without thinking, and to apologize often. That was the rock—but a wavering rock—and that in itself is a contradiction!

I note also that Peter was not above rebuking his Lord and Master. He could walk up to Jesus and rebuke Him as though they were equals. But in the next moment, he might be down on his knees in a trembling reverence, crying, "Depart from me, Lord, for I am an unclean man!"

That was Peter—more daring than any of the apostles and often with more faith—but he had more daring than he had faith! Have you met any of God's children like that?

You remember that Peter was so daring that he rushed

out of the boat and actually walked on the water, and yet he had such little faith that it would not support his daring. So he sank, and then had to be helped by the Lord to keep him from drowning!

Yes, this man Peter was the first one to confess his Lord and then the first one to deny Him.

He was the man that Jesus called "Blessed" and a little later called him Satan. "Blessed art thou, Simon Bar-Jona"; then, "Get thee behind me, Satan!"

I mention a few other contradictions about the man, Peter. He is said by a portion of the Christian church to be the vicar of Christ on earth, and yet Peter himself never seemed to have found out about it! He never referred to himself as the vicar or vice-regent of Christ; he called himself an apostle, one of the elders. That's all. The humblest elder in any Presbyterian church has a title as great as Peter ever claimed for himself, except that he said he was one of the apostles.

I could point out that Peter is supposed by many to have been the first of the popes and yet he was overshadowed by one of his fellow apostles, for without question, Paul overshadowed Peter.

The man Peter was a great man, but the man Paul was greater. It would seem to me that if God were to select a pope, the first one, He would have chosen Paul, the mightiest, the most intellectual of them all, rather than the wavering and inconsistent Peter.

I point out, too, that Peter fades out of the Book of Acts and as he does so, Paul moves in. By the time we come to the end of the Acts, Peter is not visible anywhere. Paul fills the horizon and when God would lay the foundations of His church, forming its doctrines deep and strong, He chose Paul and not Peter.

So, this is a simple and very brief sketch of the man, Peter. Many other things could be said about him, but he is able to speak to us again out of his New Testament letters for he was declared an apostle to the Jews as Paul was to the Gentiles.

The Jews had been scattered abroad and that is the reason for this letter from Peter. They had been dispersed into many nations and at the day of Pentecost, they had come back to Jerusalem, numbering into the hundreds of thousands. Then when Peter preached, they were converted in large numbers, and returning to their own countries, carried the message of the risen Saviour and the coming of the Holy Spirit. Thus there were colonies of Christians in all of the provinces of Rome and Peter felt that he was to be pastor to that great number of Jewish Christians scattered abroad. He accepted his apostleship to the Jews most seriously and he wrote his first pastoral letter to the Jewish converts to Christ scattered throughout Roman Asia.

Actually, the circumstances in the Roman provinces that brought forth this letter from Peter were very grievous indeed. The Roman emperors had begun harsh persecution of the Christians. Jesus had told them that they were to expect persecution and now it was beginning to break over their heads like billows over a sinking ship.

One of the men coming into great political power was the emperor Nero, who is remembered in history as the most incredibly wicked of all the sons of Rome. His life and his acts and his habits are among the most wretched and offensive in all of history so no one can mention in public all the crimes of which he was guilty. But he was the Emperor—and Peter and the rest of the Christians were under his control.

It is recorded of Nero that he set the city of Rome on fire and then in his own tower played the harp and sang Greek songs while Rome burned. But then he became frightened, realizing that the Romans would turn on him if they knew he had set the fire, so he looked around for a scapegoat— and who could be easier to blame than the troublesome Christians?

These believers were vocal and they were in evidence everywhere. So, Nero turned on the Christians as Hitler turned on the Jews and he had them slain by the tens of thousands. Property was taken from them, they were thrown into jail, they were tortured in many ways and they were killed—all of this throughout the regions of Bithynia and Pontus and Cappadocia and Roman Asia.

Peter, the dear man of God, knew what was happening. He had seen some of it himself in the city of Jerusalem and he knew the fury of the persecution. Out of this knowledge came his letter of encouragement, a letter inspired by the Spirit of God as he waited on the Lord in long, amazing hours of prayer for his suffering Christian brothers and sisters.

I think it must be said of Peter that within himself he felt very keenly the loneliness of the "strangers" to whom he wrote. They were scattered, they were persecuted, they were in heaviness, they were isolated in this world for their Christian faith.

The Christian, the genuine Christian, realizes that he is indeed a lonely soul in the middle of a world which affords him no fellowship. I contend that if the Christian breaks down on occasion and lets himself go in tears, he ought not to feel that he is weak. It is a normal loneliness in the midst of a world that has disowned him. He has to be a lonely man!

Those to whom Peter wrote were strangers in many ways and first of all because they were Jews. They were Jews scattered among the Romans and they never could accept and bow to the Roman ways. They learned the Greek tongue in the world of their day, but they never could learn the Roman ways. They were Jews, a people apart, even as they are today.

Besides that, they had become Christian believers so they were no longer merely Jews. Their sense of alienation from the world around them had increased and doubled. They were not only Jews—unlike the Gentiles around them—but they were Christians, unlike the Jews as well as unlike the Gentiles!

This is the reason that it is easily possible for a Christian believer to be the loneliest person in the world under a set of certain circumstances. This sense of not belonging is a part of our Christian heritage. That sense of belonging in another world and not belonging to this one steals into the Christian bosom and marks him off as being different from the people around him. Many of our hymns have been born out of that very loneliness, that sense of another and higher citizenship!

That is exactly the thing that keeps a Christian separated—knowing that his citizenship is not on earth at all but in heaven above, and that he looks for the Saviour to come. Who is there that can look more earnestly for the coming of the Lord Jesus than the one who feels that he is a lonely person in the middle of a lonely world?

Peter loved the Lord Jesus Christ and his letters to suffering believers clearly reveal that great and sweeping changes had come into his life. He had become stable, he had become solid, he had become the steady and dependable servant of Christ. Now he was able to see that suffering for Christ is one of the privileges of the Christian life and he prepared his brothers and sisters for the future with his counsel: "Beloved, think it not strange concerning the fiery trial which is to try you . . . but rejoice, inasmuch as ye are partakers of Christ's sufferings."

Fellow believers, it is the same kind of world in which we live in this twentieth century. We do well to let the Apostle Peter speak to us!

No matter who you are, no matter what your education, you can read Peter's First Epistle and understand it reasonably well and you can say to yourself, "The Holy Spirit is saying this to me!"

There isn't anything dated in the Book of God. When I go to my Bible, I find dates but no dating. I mean that I find the sense and the feeling that everything here belongs to me. There is nothing here that is obviously for another age, another time, another people.

Many other volumes and many other books of history

contain the passionate outpourings of the minds of men on local situations but we soon find ourselves bored with them. Unless we are actually doing research we do not care that much about something dated, something belonging only to another age.

But when the Holy Spirit wrote the epistles, through Peter and Paul and the rest, He wrote them and addressed them to certain people and then made them so universally applicable that every Christian who reads them today in any part of the world, in any language or dialect, forgets that they were written to someone else and says, "This was addressed to me. The Holy Spirit had me in mind. This is not antiquated and dated. This is the living Truth for me—now! It is just as though God had just heard of my trouble and is speaking to me to help me and encourage me in the time of my distress!"

Brethren, this is why the Bible stays young always. This is why the Word of the Lord God is as fresh as every new sunrise, as sweet and graciously fresh as the dew on the grass the morning after the clear night—because it is God's Word to man!

This is the wonder of divine inspiration and the wonder of the Book of God!

34

Holiness Is Not an Option

. . . as he which hath called you is holy, so be ye holy in all manner of conversation; because it is written, Be ye holy; for I am holy.

1 Peter 1:15, 16

You cannot study the Bible diligently and earnestly without being struck by an obvious fact—the whole matter of personal holiness is highly important to God!

Neither do you have to give long study to the attitudes of modern Christian believers to discern that by and large we consider the expression of true Christian holiness to be just a matter of personal option: "I have looked it over and considered it, but I don't buy it!"

I have always liked the word *exhort* better than *command* so I remind you that Peter has given every Christian a forceful exhortation to holiness of life and conversation. He clearly bases this exhortation on two great facts—first, the character of God, and second, the command of God.

His argument comes out so simply that we sophisticates stumble over it—God's children ought to be holy because God Himself is holy! We so easily overlook the fact that Peter was an apostle and he is here confronting us with the force of an apostolic injunction, completely in line with the Old Testament truth concerning the person and character of God and also in line with what the Lord Jesus had taught and revealed to His disciples and followers.

Personally, I am of the opinion that we who claim to be apostolic Christians do not have the privilege of ignoring such apostolic injunctions. I do not mean that a pastor can forbid or that a church can compel. I only mean that morally we dare not ignore this commandment, "Be ye holy."

Because it is an apostolic word, we must face up to the fact that we will have to deal with it in some way, and not ignore it—as some Christians do.

Certainly no one has provided us with an option in this matter. Who has ever given us the right or the privilege to look into the Bible and say, "I am willing to consider this matter and if I like it, I will buy it"—using the language of the day.

There is something basically wrong with our Christianity and our spirituality if we can carelessly presume that if we do not like a Biblical doctrine and choose not to "buy" it, there is no harm done.

Commandments which we have received from our Lord or from the apostles cannot be overlooked or ignored by earnest and committed Christians. God has never instructed us that we should weigh His desires for us and His commandments to us in the balances of our own judgment and then decide what we want to do about them.

A professing Christian may say, "I have found a place of real Christian freedom; these things just don't apply to me."

Of course you can walk out on it! God has given every one of us the power to make our own choices. I am not saying that we are forced to bow our necks to this yoke and we do not have to apply it to ourselves. It is true that if we do not like it, we can turn our backs on it.

The record in the New Testament is plain on this point—many people followed Jesus for a while and then walked away from Him.

Once Jesus said to His disciples: "Except ye eat my body,

my flesh, and drink my blood, there is no life in you." Many looked at one another and then walked away from Him.

Jesus turned to those remaining and said, "Will you also go away?"

Peter gave the answer which is still my answer today: "Lord, if we wanted to go away, where would we go? Thou alone hast the words of eternal life."

Those were wise words, indeed, words born of love and devotion.

So, we are not forced to obey in the Christian life, but we are forced to make a choice at many points in our spiritual maturity.

We have that power within us to reject God's instructions—but where else shall we go? If we refuse His words, which way will we turn? If we turn away from the authority of God's Word, to whose authority do we yield? Our mistake is that we generally turn to some other human—a man with breath in his nostrils.

I am old-fashioned about the Word of God and its authority. I am committed to believe that if we ignore it or consider this commandment optional, we jeopardize our souls and earn for ourselves severe judgment to come.

Now, brethren, I have said that the matter of holiness is highly important to God. I have personally counted in an exhaustive concordance and found that the word *holiness* occurs 650 times in the Bible. I have not counted words with a similar meaning in English, such as *sanctify* and *sanctified,* so the count would jump nearer to a thousand if we counted these other words with the same meaning.

This word *holy* is used to describe the character of angels, the nature of heaven and the character of God. It is written that angels are holy and those angels who gaze down upon the scenes of mankind are called the watchers and holy ones.

It is said that heaven is a holy place where no unclean thing can enter in. God Himself is described by the adjective *holy*—Holy Ghost, Holy Lord and Holy Lord God Almighty. These words are used of God throughout the Bible, showing that the highest adjective that can be ascribed to God, the highest attribute that can be ascribed to God is that of holiness, and, in a relative sense, even the angels in heaven partake of the holiness of God.

We note in the Bible, too, that the absence of holiness is given as a reason for not seeing God. I am aware of some of the grotesque interpretations which have been given to that text, "Without holiness no man shall see the Lord." My position is this: I will not throw out this Bible text just because some people have misused it to support their own patented theory about holiness. This text does have a meaning and it ought to disturb us until we have discovered what it means and how we may meet its conditions.

What does this word *holiness* really mean? Is it a negative kind of piety from which so many people have shied away?

No, of course not! Holiness in the Bible means moral wholeness—a positive quality which actually includes kindness, mercy, purity, moral blamelessness and godliness. It is always to be thought of in a positive, white intensity of degree.

Whenever it is written that God is holy it means that God is kind, merciful, pure and blameless in a white, holy intensity of degree. When used of men, it does not mean absolute holiness as it does of God, but it is still the positive intensity of the degree of holiness—and not negative.

This is why true Bible holiness is positive—a holy man can be trusted. A holy man can be tested. People who try to live by a negative standard of piety, a formula that has been copyrighted by other humans, will find that their piety does not stand up in times of difficult testing.

Genuine holiness can be put into the place of testing without fear. Whenever there is a breakdown of holiness, that is proof there never was any real degree of holiness in the first place.

Personally, I truly have been affected in my heart by

reading the testimonies and commentaries of humble men of God whom I consider to be among the great souls of Christian church history.

I have learned from them that the word and idea of holiness as originally used in the Hebrew did not have first of all the moral connotation. It did not mean that God first of all was pure, for that was taken for granted!

The original root of the word *holy* was of something beyond, something strange and mysterious and awe-inspiring. When we consider the holiness of God we talk about something heavenly, full of awe, mysterious and fear-inspiring. Now, this is supreme when it relates to God, but it is also marked in men of God and deepens as men become more like God.

It is a sense of awareness of the other world, a mysterious quality and difference that has come to rest upon some men—that is a holiness. Now, if a man should have that sense and not be morally right, then I would say that he is experiencing a counterfeit of the devil.

Whenever Satan has reason to fear a truth very gravely, he produces a counterfeit. He will try to put that truth in such a bad light that the very persons who are most eager to obey it are frightened away from it. Satan is very sly and very experienced in the forming of parodies of truth which he fears the most, and then pawns his parody off as the real thing and soon frightens away the serious-minded saints.

I regret to say that some who have called themselves by a kind of copyrighted name of holiness have allowed the doctrine to harden into a formula which has become a hindrance to repentance, for this doctrine has been invoked to cover up frivolity and covetousness, pride and worldliness.

I have seen the results. Serious, honest persons have turned away from the whole idea of holiness because of those who have claimed it and then lived selfish and conceited lives.

But, brethren, we are still under the holy authority of the apostolic command. Men of God have reminded us in the Word that God does ask us and expect us to be holy men and women of God, because we are the children of God, who is holy. The doctrine of holiness may have been badly and often wounded—but the provision of God by His pure and gentle and loving Spirit is still the positive answer for those who hunger and thirst for the life and spirit well-pleasing God.

When a good man with this special quality and mysterious Presence is morally right and walking in all the holy ways of God and carries upon himself without even knowing it the fragrance of a kingdom that is supreme above the kingdoms of this world, I am ready to accept that as being of God and from God!

By way of illustration, remember that Moses possessed these marks and qualities when he came down from the mount. He had been there with God 40 days and 40 nights—and when he came back everyone could tell where he had been. The lightning still played over his countenance, the glory of the Presence remained. This strange something which men cannot pin down or identify was there.

I lament that this mysterious quality of holy Presence has all but forsaken the earth in our day. Theologians long ago referred to it as the numinous, meaning that overplus of something that is more than righteous, but is righteous in a fearful, awe-inspiring, wondrous, heavenly sense. It is as though it is marked with a brightness, glowing with a mysterious fire.

I have commented that this latter quality has all but forsaken the earth and I think the reason is very obvious. We are men who have reduced God to our own terms. In the context of the Christian church, we are now told to "gossip" the gospel and "sell" Jesus to people!

We still talk about righteousness, but we are lacking in that bright quality, that numinous which is beyond description.

This mysterious fire was in the bush as you will remember from the Old Testament. A small fire does not frighten people unless it spreads and gets out of control. We are not afraid of fire in that sense, yet we read how Moses, kneeling beside a bush where a small fire burned, hid his face for he was afraid! He had met that mysterious quality. He was full of awe in that manifested Presence.

Later, alone in the mountain and at the sounding of a trumpet, Moses shook, and said, "I am fearfully afraid, and quake."

We are drawn again and again to that Shekinah that was over Israel for it sums up wonderfully this holiness of God's Presence. There was the overhanging cloud by day, plainly visible. It was a mysterious cloud not made of water vapor, not casting a shadow anywhere, mysterious.

As the light of day would begin to fade, that cloud began to turn incandescent and when the darkness had settled, it shone brightly like one vast light hanging over Israel.

Every tent in that diamond-shaped encampment was fully lighted by the strange Shekinah that hung over it. No man had built that fire. No one added any fuel—no one stoked or controlled it. It was God bringing Himself within the confines of the human eye and shining down in His Presence over Israel.

I can imagine a mother taking her little child by the hand to walk through the encampment.

I am sure she would kneel down and whisper to that little fellow: "I want to show you something wonderful, Look! Look at that!"

Probably the response would be: "What is it, Mama?"

Then she would reply in a hushed voice: "That is God—God is there! Our leader Moses saw that fire in the bush. Later, he saw that fire in the mountain. Since we left Egypt that fire of God has followed us and hovered over us all through these years."

"But how do you know it is God, Mama?"

"Because of the Presence in that fire, the mysterious Presence from another world."

This Shekinah, this Presence, had no particular connotation of morality for Israel—that was all taken for granted. It did hold the connotation and meaning of reverence and awe, the solemn and inspiring, different and wonderful and glorious—all of that was there as it was also in the temple.

Then it came down again at Pentecost—that same fire sitting upon each of them—and it rested upon them with an invisible visibility. If there had been cameras, I do not think those tongues of fire could have been photographed—but they were there. It was the sense of being in or surrounded by this holy element, and so strong was it that in Jerusalem when the Christians gathered on Solomon's porch, the people stood off from them as wolves will stand away from a bright camp fire. They looked on, but the Bible says "they durst not join themselves to them."

Why? Were they held back by any prohibiton or restriction?

No one had been warned not to come near these praying people, humble and harmless, clean and undefiled. But the crowd could not come. They could not rush in and trample the place down. They stood away from Solomon's porch because they had sensed a holy quality, a mysterious and holy Presence within this company of believers.

Later, when Paul wrote to the Corinthian Christians to explain the mysterious fullness of the Holy Spirit of God, he said: "Some of you, when you meet together and you hear and obey God, know there is such a sense of God's presence that the unbelievers fall on their faces and then go out and report that God is with you indeed."

Now, that kind of Presence emanates from God as all holiness emanates from God.

If we are what we ought to be in Christ and by His Spirit, if the whole sum of our lives beginning with the inner life is becoming more Godlike and Christlike, I believe something of that divine and mysterious quality and Presence will be upon us.

I have met a few of God's saints who appeared to have this holy brightness upon them, but they did not know it because of their humility and gentleness of spirit. I do not hesitate to confess that my fellowship with them has meant more to me than all of the teaching I have ever received. I do stand deeply indebted to every Bible teacher I have had through the years, but they did little but instruct my head. The brethren I have known who had this strange and mysterious quality and awareness of God's Person and Presence instructed my heart.

Do we understand what a gracious thing it is to be able to say of a man, a brother in the Lord, "He is truly a man of God"? He doesn't have to tell us that, but he lives quietly and confidently day by day with the sense of this mysterious, awe-inspiring Presence that comes down on some people and means more than all the glib tongues in the world!

Actually, I am afraid of all the glib tongues. I am afraid of the man who can always flip open his Bible and answer every question—he knows too much! I am afraid of the man who has thought it all out and has a dozen epigrams he can quote, the answers which he has throught up over the years to settle everything spiritual. Brethren, I'm afraid of it!

There is a silence that can be more eloquent than all human speech. Sometimes there is a confusion of face and bowing of the head that speaks more divine truth than the most eloquent preacher can impart.

So, Peter reminds us that it is the Lord who has said: "Be ye holy as I am holy, and because I am holy."

First, bring your life into line morally so that God can make it holy; then bring your spiritual life into line that God may settle upon you with the Holy Ghost—with that quality of the Wonderful and the Mysterious and the Divine.

You do not cultivate it and you do not even know it, but it is there and it is this quality of humility invaded by the Presence of God which the church of our day lacks. Oh, that we might yearn for the knowledge and Presence of God in our lives from moment to moment, so that without human cultivation and without toilsome seeking there would come upon us this enduement that gives meaning to our witness! It is a sweet and radiant fragrance and I suggest that in some of our churches it may be strongly sensed and felt.

Now that I have said that, I had better stop and predict that some will ask me. "You don't go by your feelings, do you, Mr. Tozer?"

Well, I do not dismiss the matter of feeling and you can quote me on that if it is worth it!

Feeling is an organ of knowledge and I do not hesitate to say so. Feeling is an organ of knowledge.

To develop this, will you define the word *love* for me?

I don't believe you can actually define love—you can describe it but you cannot define it. A person or a group of people or a race which has never heard of the word *love* can never come to an understanding of what love is even if they could memorize the definitions in all of the world's dictionaries.

But just consider what happens to any simple, freckle-faced boy with his big ears and his red hair awry when he first falls in love and the feeling of it comes into every part of his being. All at once he knows more about love than all of the dictionaries put together!

This is what I am saying—love can only be understood by the feeling of it. The same is true with the warmth of the sun. Tell a man who has no feeling that it is a warm day and he will never understand what you mean. But take a normal man who is out in the warm sun and he will soon know it is warm. You can know more about the sun by feeling than you can by description.

So there are qualities in God that can never be explained to the intellect and can only be known by the heart, the innermost being. That is why I say that I do believe in feeling. I believe in what the old writers called religious affection—and we have so little of it because we have not laid the groundwork for it. The groundwork is repentance and obedience and separation and holy living!

I am confident that whenever this groundwork is laid, there will come to us this sense of the other-worldly Presence of God and it will become wonderfully, wonderfully real.

I have at times heard an expression in our prayers, "Oh, God, draw feelingly near!"

I don't think that is too far off—in spite of those who can only draw back and sit in judgment.

"Oh, God, come feelingly near!" God drew feelingly near to Moses in the bush and on the mount. He came feelingly near to the church at Pentecost and He came feelingly near to that Corinthian church when the unbelievers went away awe-struck to report that "God is really in their midst!"

I am willing to confess in humility that we need this in our day.

35

Husband and Wife: A Partnership!

Likewise, ye wives, be in subjection to your own husbands.... husbands, dwell with them according to knowledge; giving honor unto the wife ... whose adorning ... the ornament of a meek and quiet spirit.

1 Peter 3:1-7

We have come to a sorry time in history when public speakers—including many preachers—see fit to deal with problems between men and women, husbands and wives, as a kind of humor calling for a bushel of laughs.

Throughout man's existence, the biological positions of the two sexes have remained unchanged, but the psychological attitudes and the social relations have been altered radically from time to time.

In recent years there has been a positive and radical revolution with respect to the relationships of the sexes and I think its origins can largely be traced in the United States. It is an impossibility for me to analyze here the impetus and the details of this movement which has been widely acclaimed as seeking "liberation" for women of the world.

What I do want to say about the relationships of husbands and wives will boil down to this: for the Christian of either sex, there is only one rule to follow and that is, "What does the Bible say?"

Christians are first of all children of God, and as children of God we are committed to the Word of God. We are committed to a Man and a Book, the man being the Lord Jesus Christ and the book, of course, the Holy Scriptures.

When we have discovered what the Bible has to say with finality about any subject and have determined what pleases the Man in the glory, there is no room left for argument.

In this epistle, Peter makes a plain statement that Christian wives ought to be in subjection to their own husbands, enforcing what the Bible seems to teach in other places— that the man as head of the race is head of the home.

Go back to Genesis and you will find that God made Adam from the dust of the ground and blew the breath of life into his nostrils. Then, because it was not good for him to be alone, God made the woman from a part of the man—and the woman must understand and accept that.

But, quickly and on the other hand, it must be said that there is absolutely no scriptural authority, neither precept nor biblical example, to allow any husband to behave as a brutal lord, ruling his home with an iron hand.

Read again the story of Abraham and Sarah and you will note the noble leadership of the man Abraham. He never ruled with an iron hand!

Go on to poor Jacob with all of his domestic difficulties. There was always a graciousness and a kindness within his family circle!

You can continue through Old Testament history and although it was a bit in the shadows compared with the New Testament, still and nevertheless, there was never any brutal masculine domination in the families with whom God was dealing.

In your serious study of the Bible as the Word of God, you will have to agree that the Bible seems to teach that the husband and wife should supplement one another. In other words, it seems to be the will of God that husband and wife together may become what neither one could be apart and alone!

Certainly the Bible picture is plain in denying the husband any right to be a dominating despot delighting in hard-handed dealings with his wife and family.

On the other hand, neither is a dominating and rebellious wife ever recognized nor approved in the scriptures!

An overwhelming and mischievous wife is the product of sin and unbelief and such a role has no place whatsoever in the will of God for the Christian family.

Actually, I think we may interpret the scriptures as teaching that God never intended there should be a continuing rivalry and competition between husbands and wives. Rather, it teaches the ideals of understanding and cooperation.

There is to be the understanding that two people have entered into a covenant by their choice and by force of circumstance, living in the same home and situation. The understanding should include the fact that the husband, according to the scripture and the will of God, is the head of the race and the home, but that he should function wisely, according to Peter's gentle admonition: "Ye husbands, dwell with them according to knowledge."

Peter is advising the husband to use his head and the common sense he has been given: ". . . giving honour unto the wife, as unto the weaker vessel, and as being heirs together of the grace of life."

In other words, husband and wife are children of God together, equal heirs of the grace of life.

If we will remember this fact prayerfully, I think we will become aware that it is at this point that chivalry was born! I am speaking of Christian chivalry, as we understand it.

The world in which we live and the society of which we are a part have often sought to lampoon and satirize the concept of woman as the weaker vessel. There have been thousands of jokes, and cartoonists have had a field day with their drawings of the buxom woman leading the meek, little lamb-of-a-man down the street.

But we remember that the scriptures say that the man and the woman are heirs together of the grace of life. Husband and wife, if both are Christians, are Christian heirs together! They are united in their strongest bond—they are one in Jesus Christ, their Saviour!

Now, Peter makes a very strong comment in this passage for the benefit of husbands.

"Husbands, your prayers will be hindered if you do not give honour unto the wife, as unto the weaker vessel. . ."

I suppose there are many Christian husbands whose prayers are not being answered and they can think up lots of reasons. But the fact is that thoughtless husbands are simply big, overbearing clods when it comes to consideration of their wives.

If the husband would get himself straightened out in his own mind and spirit and live with his wife according to knowledge, and treat her with the chivalry that belongs to her as the weaker vessel, remembering that she is actually his sister in Christ, his prayers would be answered in spite of the devil and all of the other reasons that he gives.

A husband's spiritual problems do not lie in the Kremlin nor in the Vatican but in the heart of the man himself—in his attitude and inability to resist the temptation to grumble and growl and dominate!

There is no place for that kind of male rulership in any Christian home. What the Bible calls for is proper and kindly recognition of the true relationships of understanding and love, and the acceptance of a spirit of cooperation between the husband and wife.

Peter also seeks to give us a plain answer in this passage concerning the life and conduct of a Christian wife who has an unbelieving and scornful husband.

We dare not deal with this only as a problem out of ancient history. In all of our congregations, we do face the question of the Christian wife: "How do I adjust my Christian life so that I can be obedient to the scriptures while I am living with a man who hates God and showers me with grumbling and abuse when I insist that I am going to God's house?"

First, we must admit that there is the kind of woman who talks about praying for her husband, but she will never live to see him converted because she refuses the scriptural position that God has given her, and more bluntly, because her husband has never seen any spiritual characteristics in her life that he would want for himself!

Peter could hardly give Christian wives any plainer counsel: "Be in subjection to your own husbands; that, if any obey not the word, they also may without the word be won by the conversation of the wives; while they behold your chaste conversation coupled with fear."

The scriptural advice is to this effect: that the quiet, cooperative Christian wife is a powerful instrument for good in the home, and without too many words, is still an evangelist hard to resist. Peter strongly infers that the man, seemingly rejecting her doctrine and laughing at her faith, is badly smitten deep in his own conscience by her meek and quiet spirit and her chaste conversation coupled with godly fear.

In summary, we have mentioned two extremes—the harsh husband whose prayers are not answered, and the wife whose life does not show consistent godliness and patience in adversity.

I thank God that in between those two positions there are great throngs of good, decent people trying to do the best they can for God in their life situations, overlooking the obvious irritations and together experiencing the grace of God!

I thank God indeed for that great number of believing men and women who get along together in Christ's bonds and with the help of the Spirit of God succeed in establishing a consistent example to their families, their neighbors and their friends!

I am aware that at about this point some of you are

wondering if I will ignore the rest of Peter's admonition to the Christian women of his day.

There is a problem in this passage, but I may die tomorrow and I would not want to die knowing that only a day before I had been too cowardly and timid to deal with a text of scripture!

Here it is, in Peter's counsel to the wives:

"Whose adorning let it not be that outward adorning of plaiting the hair, and of wearing of gold, or of putting on of apparel; but let it be the hidden man of the heart."

First, notice the manner which Peter lifts the entire questions up and beyond the plane where there is division between the sexes and puts the matter on a spiritual plane where there is no division and where it is the hidden being of the heart and the spirit that really matters.

Second, what does the Bible really teach here about the outward adorning and dress. Does it expressly forbid the plaiting of the hair, the wearing of gold and the putting on of apparel? This is a question often asked.

Let's say "yes" and then go on from there and see where we stand.

When I was a boy they used to call plaiting of the hair "braiding." Every little girl had a pigtail that came to her hips. The longer the pigtail the prouder the girl!

My sister used to wear braided hair and that's what it means—exactly what plaited hair once meant in England.

Does the Bible say, then, that a woman must not be adorned with braided hair?

If we say, "Yes, that's what it means"—that rules out the braiding of your hair.

The advice continues: "Let it not be the wearing of gold."

Does that mean that gold can never be worn in any way by a Christian woman?

We will agree for the moment and say that gold is out!

"Nor the putting on of apparel."

Now, wait a minute! We are in trouble with our reason-

...ng here, because this certainly does not mean that the woman is not to put on any apparel.

If it doesn't mean a strict ban on fixing the hair or wearing of gold or putting on of apparel, what does it mean?

 It means the true attractiveness of the person is not outward but inward! Therefore, the Christian woman should remember that she cannot buy true attractiveness—that radiance which really shines forth in beauty is of the heart and spirit and not of the body!

That is what Peter meant and anything else by way of exclusion or structure is of narrow, private interpretation and will lead into an unloving fanaticism!

There is not one line of expression here that would lead us to believe that Peter was laying down the law that it is wrong for a woman to braid her hair. The women know they have to do something with it!

Nor is there anything in the scripture that teaches that the use of gold is forbidden in proper ways. God in creation made gold and strung it all around. It is pretty to look at and it is an element in itself. If we have any of it and can afford it, there is nothing in the scripture that says "Don't wear it" any more than it says, "Don't wear apparel!"

So, the teaching is plain: don't let your apparel be your true attractiveness. Don't try to substitute gold or jewelry for the true beauty of the being!

I am sure that we would not be mistaken to presume that Peter had a reason for writing this, for history bears out the fact that there were customs and fads and styles in those days, too.

I suppose it was the vogue and the thing to do—make the braided hair a kind of work of art, with great displays of gold and jewelry and fine apparel among the worldly and unsaved women of that pagan time.

Perhaps Peter sounds a trifle sour to some when he writes and says, "You Christian women are a different kind of person than you were before you knew the Lord. As Christians you should be more interested in character and inward spiritual life than in your clothing and adornment."

Having said this about the true inward attractiveness of the person, it must also be said that no Christian woman should ever sink into slovenly habits of dress and appearance. How can it be possible for any Christian woman, carrying her big Bible and teacher's quarterly, to become known as a proverbial "dowd"?

She cannot impress me with her professed spirituality. I can only shrug and think about her unkempt dress: "Did she go to the old bureau in the attic and pull out the old rag or did she sleep in it?"

I can be very positive about this—I don't believe that true spirituality can afford to leave that kind of slovenly impression. There is no place in the heart of Jesus Christ nor in that of the tender, artistic Holy Ghost for dowdiness nor dirt nor inconsistency!

I remember the account of the old Quaker brother who had to make a call at the home of one of the Christian sisters in his city.

They greeted one another in the traditional dignified manner of the Quakers and then had a brief conversation about the things of God.

As he was about to leave, she said, "Brother, would you care to pray with me before you go?"

He said, "No," and she said, "Why?"

He answered, "Your house is dirty and God never told me to get down on my knees in a dirty house. Clean up your house and I will come back and pray."

Perhaps she had been too busy praying to keep the house clean, but I believe an orderly and well-kept house would have helped her Christian testimony, and perhaps she could have prayed better, as well.

Now, there has to be some sort of outward adorning and I would summarize it in four familiar words: *clean, neat, modest, appropriate.*

None can say that they do not understand the word

clean. However poor we may be, we may still be clean. Nearly everyone has enough water available for basic cleanliness.

Why can't we all be neat in our daily contacts? I do not think anyone ever needs to look as though he had gone through a cyclone and had no time since to get "accumulated."

In our day, some folks seem to think the word *modest* is a comical word. You can laugh it off if you want to, but it is one of the words that we will face in that great day of coming judgment.

In our Christian lives, we should know the strength of the word *appropriate*. I think every Christian woman should dress appropriately, properly and suitably to her circumstances and to her income. A Christian woman who tries to give out tracts dressed in loud, flashy apparel or in dirty and disheveled garb will be a poor advertisement for the gospel she is trying to proclaim publicly!

I realize that some women excuse their manner of dress in public by the fact that they have so little money to spend for clothing.

I contend that a woman still doesn't have to be grotesque in her garb even though she must wrestle with the problems of small income.

You know that I ride the public busses occasionally and for the small price of the fare it is a wonderful place to observe human nature.

When I see some of the inappropriate and grotesque things worn by women boarding the busses I have wondered why others in the family did not protest: "Please, Mama, don't go out like that! People will think you have escaped . . ."

I think there is a great contradiction apparent among us. Many women are working so hard in all kinds of jobs that they are making themselves old in the effort to get money enough to buy the clothes and cosmetics that are supposed to make them look young.

As far as I am concerned, it does not reflect any credit on the common sense or spirituality of any woman who knowingly goes beyond her financial bracket to decorate herself for the sake of appearance!

Finally, I think that a Christian woman must be careful about the kind of person she sets up as a model of character and example in daily life. It is a sad thing to have our minds occupied with the wrong kind of people.

I don't think English history books will ever report that Suzanna Wesley was one of the best-dressed women of her day or that she ever received a medal for social activity. But she was the mother of Charles and John Wesley, those princes of Christian song and theology. She taught her own family, and her spiritual life and example have placed her name high in God's hall of fame for all eternity.

So, if you want to take models to follow day by day, please do not take the artificial, globe-trotting females who are intent only upon themselves, their careers and their publicity. Rather, take Sara, the princess who gave her love and obedience to Abraham; or Suzanna Wesley or Florence Nightingale, Clara Barton or Mary Fuller.

There are so many good examples and it is a serious matter, for the judgment shall declare every person's faith and work and influence!

I have not been trying here just to fill the role of a feminine counselor, but to remind you that the Apostle Peter, a great man of God, said it all a long time ago! True adorning is the lasting beauty that is within. It is the glowing but hidden being of the heart, more radiant than all of the jewels that one can buy!

God help us all, men and women of whatever marital, social or domestic status, that we may do the will of God and thus win our crown!

36

Who Put Jesus on the Cross?

He was wounded for our transgressions, he was bruised for our iniquities: the chastisement of our peace was upon him; and with his stripes we are healed.

Isa. 53:5

There is a strange conspiracy of silence in the world today—even in religious circles—about man's responsibility for sin, the reality of judgment, and about an outraged God and the necessity for a crucified Saviour.

On the other hand, there is an open and powerful movement swirling throughout the world designed to give people peace of mind in relieving them of any historical responsibility for the trial and crucifixion of Jesus Christ. The problem with modern decrees and pronouncements in the name of brotherhood and tolerance is their basic misconception of Christian theology.

A great shadow lies upon every man and every woman—the fact that our Lord was bruised and wounded and crucified for the entire human race. This is the basic human responsibility that men are trying to push off and evade.

Let us not eloquently blame Judas nor Pilate. Let us not curl our lips at Judas and accuse, "He sold Him for money!"

Let us pity Pilate, the weak-willed, because he did not

have courage enough to stand for the innocency of the man whom he declared had done no wrong.

Let us not curse the Jews for delivering Jesus to be crucified. Let us not single out the Romans in blaming them for putting Jesus on the cross.

Oh, they were guilty, certainly! But they were our accomplices in crime. They and we put Him on the cross, not they alone. That rising malice and anger that burns so hotly in your breast today put Him there. That basic dishonesty that comes to light in your being when you knowingly cheat and chisel on your income tax return—that put Him on the cross. The evil, the hatred, the suspicion, the jealousy, the lying tongue, the carnality, the fleshly love of pleasure—all of these in natural man joined in putting Him on the cross.

We may as well admit it. Everyone of us in Adam's race had a share in putting Him on the cross!

I have often wondered how any professing Christian man or woman could approach the communion table and participate in the memorial of our Lord's death without feeling and sensing the pain and the shame of the inward confession: "I, too, am among those who helped put Him on the cross!"

I remind you that it is characteristic of the natural man to keep himself so busy with unimportant trifles that he is able to avoid the settling of the most important matters relating to life and existence.

Men and women will gather anywhere and everywhere to talk about and discuss every subject from the latest fashions on up to Plato and philosophy—up and down the scale. They talk about the necessity for peace. They may talk about the church and how it can be a bulwark against communism. None of these things are embarrassing subjects.

But the conversation all stops and the taboo of silence becomes effective when anyone dares to suggest that there are spiritual subjects of vital importance to our souls that ought to be discussed and considered. There seems to be an unwritten rule in polite society that if any religious subjects are to be discussed, it must be within the framework of theory—"never let it get personal!"

All the while, there is really only one thing that is of vital and lasting importance—the fact that our Lord Jesus Christ "was wounded for our transgressions; he was bruised for our iniquities; the chastisement of our peace was upon him; and with his stripes we are healed."

There are two very strong and terrible words here—*transgressions* and *iniquities*.

A *transgression* is a breaking away, a revolt from just authority. In all of the moral universe, only man and the fallen angels have rebelled and violated the authority of God, and men are still in flagrant rebellion against that authority.

There is no expression in the English language which can convey the full weight and force of terror inherent in the words *transgression* and *iniquity*. But in man's fall and transgression against the created order and authority of God we recognize perversion and twistedness and deformity and crookedness and rebellion. These are all there, and, undeniably, they reflect the reason and the necessity for the death of Jesus Christ on the cross.

The word *iniquity* is not a good word—and God knows how we hate it! But the consequences of iniquity cannot be escaped.

The prophet reminds us clearly that the Saviour was bruised for "our iniquities."

We deny it and say, "No!" but the fingerprints of all mankind are plain evidence against us. The authorities have no trouble finding and apprehending the awkward burglar who leaves his fingerprints on tables and doorknobs, for they have his record. So, the fingerprints of man are found in every dark cellar and in every alley and in every dimly-lighted evil place throughout the world—every man's fingerprints are recorded and God knows man

from man. It is impossible to escape our guilt and place
our moral responsibilities upon someone else. It is a highly
personal matter—"our iniquities."

For our iniquities and our transgressions He was bruised
and wounded. I do not even like to tell you of the implications of His wounding. It really means that He was profaned and broken, stained and defiled. He was Jesus Christ
when men took Him into their evil hands. Soon He was
humiliated and profaned. They plucked out His beard. He
was stained with His own blood, defiled with earth's
grime. Yet He accused no one and He cursed no one. He
was Jesus Christ, the wounded one.

Israel's great burden and amazing blunder was her
judgment that this wounded one on the hillside beyond
Jerusalem was being punished for His own sin.

The prophet foresaw this historic error in judgment, and
he himself was a Jew, saying: "We thought He was smitten
of God. We thought that God was punishing Him for His
own iniquity for we did not know then that God was
punishing Him for our transgressions and our iniquities."

He was profaned for our sakes. He who is the second
person of the Godhead was not only wounded for us, but
He was profaned by ignorant and unworthy men.

Isaiah reported that "the chastisement of our peace was
upon him."

How few there are who realize that it is this peace—
the health and prosperity and welfare and safety of the
individual—which restores us to God. A chastisement fell
upon Him so that we as individual humans could experience peace with God if we so desired. But the chastisement
was upon Him. Rebuke, discipline and correction—these
are found in chastisement. He was beaten and scourged in
public by the decree of the Romans. They lashed Him in
public view as they later lashed Paul. They whipped and
punished Him in full view of the jeering public, and His
bruised and bleeding and swollen person was the answer
to the peace of the world and to the peace of the human

heart. He was chastised for our peace; the blows fell upon Him.

I do not suppose there is any more humiliating punishment ever devised by mankind than that of whipping and flogging grown men in public view. Many men who have been put in a jail have become a kind of hero in the eye of the public. Heavy fines have been assessed against various offenders of the law, but it is not unusual for such an offender to boast and brag about his escape. But when a bad man is taken out before a laughing, jeering crowd, stripped to the waist and soundly whipped like a child—a bad child—he loses face and has no boasting left. He will probably never be the bold, bad man he was before. That kind of whipping and chastisement breaks the spirit and humiliates. The chagrin is worse than the lash that falls on the back.

I speak for myself as a forgiven and justified sinner, and I think I speak for a great host of forgiven and born-again men and women, when I say that in our repentance we sensed just a fraction and just a token of the wounding and chastisement which fell upon Jesus Christ as He stood in our place and in our behalf. A truly penitent man who has realized the enormity of his sin and rebellion against God senses a violent revulsion against himself—he does not feel that he can actually dare to ask God to let him off. But peace has been established, for the blows have fallen on Jesus Christ—publicly humiliated and disgraced as a common thief, wounded and bruised and bleeding under the lash for sins He did not commit; for rebellions in which He had no part; for iniquity in the human stream that was an outrage to a loving God and Creator.

Isaiah sums up his message of a substitutionary atonement with the good news that "with his stripes we are healed."

The meaning of these "stripes" in the original language is not a pleasant description. It means to be actually hurt and injured until the entire body is black and blue as one great bruise. Mankind has always used this kind of bodily laceration as a punitive measure. Society has always insisted upon the right to punish a man for his own wrongdoing. The punishment is generally suited to the nature of the crime. It is a kind of revenge—society taking vengeance against the person who dared flout the rules.

But the suffering of Jesus Christ was not punitive. It was not for Himself and not for punishment of anything that He Himself had done.

The suffering of Jesus was corrective. He was willing to suffer in order that He might correct us and perfect us, so that His suffering might not begin and end in suffering, but that it might begin in suffering and end in healing.

Brethren, that is the glory of the cross! That is the glory of the kind of sacrifice that was for so long in the heart of God! That is the glory of the kind of atonement that allows a repentant sinner to come into peaceful and gracious fellowship with his God and Creator! It began in His suffering and it ended in our healing. It began in His wounds and ended in our purification. It began in His bruises and ended in our cleansing.

What is our repentance? I discover that repentance is mainly remorse for the share we had in the revolt that wounded Jesus Christ, our Lord. Further, I have discovered that truly repentant men never quite get over it, for repentance is not a state of mind and spirit that takes its leave as soon as God has given forgiveness and as soon as cleansing is realized.

That painful and acute conviction that accompanies repentance may well subside and a sense of peace and cleansing come, but even the holiest of justified men will think back over his part in the wounding and the chastisement of the Lamb of God. A sense of shock will still come over him. A sense of wonder will remain—wonder that the Lamb that was wounded should turn His wounds into the cleansing and forgiveness of one who wounded Him.

This brings to mind a gracious moving in many of our

evangelical church circles—a willingness to move toward the spiritual purity of heart taught and exemplified so well by John Wesley in a time of spiritual dryness.

In spite of the fact that the word *sanctification* is a good Bible word, we have experienced a period in which evangelical churches hardly dared breathe the word because of the fear of being classified among the "holy rollers."

Not only is the good word *sanctification* coming back, but I am hopeful that what the word stands for in the heart and mind of God is coming back, too. The believing Christian, the child of God, should have a holy longing and desire for the pure heart and clean hands that are a delight to his Lord. It was for this that Jesus Christ allowed Himself to be humiliated, maltreated, lacerated. He was bruised, wounded and chastised so that the people of God could be a cleansed and spiritual people—in order that our minds might be pure and our thoughts pure. This provision all began in His suffering and ends in our cleansing. It began with His open, bleeding wounds and ends in peaceful hearts and calm and joyful demeanor in His people.

Every humble and devoted believer in Jesus Christ must have his own periods of wonder and amazement at this mystery of godliness—the willingness of the Son of Man to take our place in judgment and in punishment. If the amazement has all gone out of it, something is wrong, and you need to have the stony ground broken up again!

I often remind you that Paul, one of the holiest men who ever lived, was not ashamed of his times of remembrance and wonder over the grace and kindness of God. He knew that God did not hold his own sins against him forever. Knowing the account was all settled, Paul's happy heart assured him again and again that all was well. At the same time, Paul could only shake his head in amazement, and confess: "I am unworthy to be called, but by His grace, I am a new creation in Jesus Christ!"

I make this point about the faith and assurance and rejoicing of Paul in order to say that if that humble sense of

perpetual penance ever leaves our justified being, we are
on the way to backsliding.

Charles Finney, one of the greatest of all of God's men
throughout the years, testified that in the midst of his
labors and endeavors in bringing men to Christ, he would
at times sense a coldness in his own heart.

Finney did not excuse it. In his writings he told of having
to turn from all of his activities, seeking God's face and
Spirit anew in fasting and prayer.

"I plowed up until I struck fire and met God," he wrote.
What a helpful and blessed formula for the concerned children of God in every generation!

Those who compose the Body of Christ, His church,
must be inwardly aware of two basic facts if we are to be
joyfully effective for our Lord.

We must have the positive knowledge that we are clean
through His wounds, with God's peace realized through
His stripes. This is how God assures us that we may be all
right inside. In this spiritual condition, we will treasure the
purity of His cleansing and we will not excuse any evil or
wrong-doing.

Also, we must keep upon us a joyful and compelling
sense of gratitude for the bruised and wounded One, our
Lord Jesus Christ. Oh, what a mystery of redemption—
that the bruises of One healed the bruises of many; that the
wounds of One healed the wounds of millions; that the
stripes of One healed the stripes of many.

The wounds and bruises that should have fallen upon us
fell upon Him, and we are saved for His sake!

Many years ago, an historic group of Presbyterians were
awed by the wonder and the mystery of Christ's having
come in the flesh to give Himself as an offering for every
man's sin.

Those humble Christians said to one another: "Let us
walk softly and search our hearts and wait on God and
seek His face throughout the next three months. Then we
will come to the communion table with our hearts

prepared—lest the table of our Lord should become a common and careless thing."

God still seeks humble, cleansed and trusting hearts through which to reveal His divine power and grace and life. A professional botanist from the university can describe the acacia bush of the desert better than Moses could ever do—but God is still looking for the humble souls who are not satisfied until God speaks with the divine fire in the bush.

A research scientist could be employed to stand and tell us more about the elements and properties found in bread and wine than the apostles ever knew. But this is our danger: we may have lost the light and warmth of the Presence of God, and we may have only bread and wine. The fire will have gone from the bush, and the glory will not be in our act of communion and fellowship.

It is not so important that we know all of the history and all of the scientific facts, but it is vastly important that we desire and know and cherish the Presence of the Living God, who has given Jesus Christ to be the propitiation for our sins; and not for ours only, but also for the sins of the whole world.

37

What Is the Supreme Sin of a Profane Society

He was in the world, and the world was made by him, and the world knew him not.

John 1:10

The Bible tells us in a variety of ways of an ancient curse that lingers with us to this very hour—the willingness of human society to be completely absorbed in a godless world!

It is still the supreme sin of unregenerate man that, even though Jesus Christ has come into the world, he cannot feel His all-pervading Presence, he cannot see the true Light, and he cannot hear His Voice of love and entreaty!

We have become a "profane" society—absorbed and intent with nothing more than the material and physical aspects of this earthly life. Men and women glory in the fact that they are now able to live in unaccustomed luxury in expensive homes; that they can trade in shiny and costly automobiles on shinier and more costly automobiles every year; and that their tailored suits and silk and satin dresses represent an expenditure never before possible in a society of common working people.

This is the curse that lies upon modern man—he is insensible and blind and deaf in his eagerness to forget that there is a God, in his strange belief that materialism and humanism constitute the "good life."

My fellow man, do you not know that your great sin is this: the all-pervading and eternal Presence is here, and you cannot feel Him?

Are you not aware that there is a great and true Light which brightly shines—and you cannot see it?

Have you not heard within your being a tender Voice whispering of the eternal value of your soul—and yet you have said, "I have heard nothing"?

This is, in essence, the charge that John levels at human kind: Jesus Christ, the Word of God, was in the world, and the world failed to recognize Him.

Now, our word *world* in the English needs a bit of definition. In the Bible it has three distinct meanings, and two of them concern us in this passage in John's Gospel. *World* here means nature and mankind—both coming from the very same Greek word. They are used together without clear distinction, so that when the Bible says, "He was in the world, and the world knew him not," the two meanings are apparent. You must check the context to learn which meaning is which, because they come from a precise word in the original.

In the Bible, the word *world* comes from a root word meaning to tend and take care of and provide for. Then, it also means an orderly arrangement plus a decoration.

As far as I am concerned, everywhere I look in His world I see God and my soul is delighted. I look into a dry, old book that looks like a telephone directory gone mad—we call it a lexicon—and I find that in the New Testament the word *world* means "an orderly arranged system, highly decorative, which is tended, cared for, looked after and provided for." It is all there in that one word.

Anyone who knows God, even slightly, would expect God to make an orderly world because God Himself is the essence of order. God was never the author of disorder—whether it be in society, in the home, or in the mind or body of man.

I have noticed that some people let themselves go to

seed in a number of ways, thinking it makes them more spiritual—but I disagree. I think it is proper to comb your hair, if you have any. I do not think it is a mark of deep inward spirituality for a man to forget that a soiled shirt is easily cleaned and that baggy trousers were originally meant to have an orderly crease in them. I am sure God is not grieved when His Christian children take a little time every day to present themselves in clean and orderly appearance.

Some of the saints of God also insist upon completely informal and spontaneous worship. I do not think our Lord is grieved by a service of worship in which we know what we are going to sing—because God is a God of order.

So the word *world* has this idea of order in it, and we can expect God to be orderly because it is necessary to His nature. The world is a mathematical world and the essence of mathematics is order—it has to be that way.

Those who have gone on to know God better will also expect that God would make a beautiful world and that is exactly what the Bible teaches. God has made an orderly and beautiful world, and He is looking after it, providing for it, and tending it.

I think this is a delightful thing—God can take an old, dry word which has been dead for hundreds of years and speak to the bones and they get up and stand and sing a solo. That is what God has done here with the word *world*.

You will think about this the next time you are asked to sing: "For the beauty of the earth, For the glory of the skies, / For the love which from our birth over and around us lies, / Lord of all, to Thee we raise This our hymn of grateful praise. / For the wonder of each hour Of the day and of the night, / Hill and vale, and tree and flower, Sun and moon, and stars of light, / Lord of all, to Thee we raise This our hymn of grateful praise."

Let me tell you that the man who wrote that was not simply having himself a poetical time. He was putting in harmonious language a truth—and that truth is that God made a world beautiful in its order.

At this point I anticipate a word of argument from Mr. Worldly Wiseman, the man who has more brains than he has heart, who thinks more than he prays, and who tries to understand and measure the unapproachable glory of God with his poor little peanut head.

He is likely to say, "Now, wait a minute. You are talking about God making the world so beautiful, but don't you know that *beauty* is a word only—a word we use to describe that which happens to please us? If a person likes the way something looks, he says it is beautiful. On the other hand, if we don't like the way something looks, we say it is ugly. So, nothing is beautiful or ugly in itself—it just depends upon whether we happen to like it or not!"

So, Mr. Worldly Wiseman tells us that this idea that God made a beautiful world is all wrong. He is of the opinion that such an idea is only the figment of an over-heated religious imagination.

Frankly, Mr. Worldly Wiseman does not frighten me by his learned criticism and I am not looking for a place to hide, because I think that he is the dumb one, after all.

Listen, brethren. God made us in His image and in His own likeness and there is a similarity between the minds of men and the mind of God, sin being excepted. Take sin out of the mind of man and the similarity to God is there because God made man in His image. I repeat—if the human race would only see that God made us in His image, we would stop wallowing in the gutter and try to behave like God ordained when He made us in His own image and likeness.

When He made us in His image, part of that was mental and aesthetic so that my mind is somewhat like God's mind as soon as I get sin out of it. There is no doubt that when God makes a thing beautiful and orderly, it pleases the mind of God.

I say that it is only a half-educated man who insists that *beauty* is only a word that we give to something that happens to please us. The simple fact is that God made things to please Himself and for His pleasure they are and were created. Why should we apologize because we have the God-given ability to like what God likes and to be pleased with that which pleases God?

Now, I think that God first makes things orderly for utility. Whenever He made something in this universe it was because He had a purpose for it. I do not believe there is anything in the universe that just got here by accident. Everything in the universe has a meaning.

My father was philosophical about many things and I remember that he used to sit during the summertime and ponder why God made the mosquitoes. I still do not have the answer, but I am just a human being, and just because I do not have that answer, I am not going to accuse the Creator of making a cosmic blunder. I know the mosquito is not a blunder—he is just a pest. But God made him.

The same principle is true of a great many other things. I do not know why God does some things, but I am convinced that nothing is accidental in His universe. The fact that we do not know the reason behind some things is not basis enough for us to call them divine accidents.

If I am allowed to go into an operating room in a hospital, I find many strange and complex things all around me. I am completely ignorant as to what most of them are and how they are supposed to be used. But the surgeon knows—and all of those tools and instruments are not there by accident.

If I could step into the cab of one of the great, powerful diesel locomotives, I would be perplexed and confused trying to figure out why there are so many buttons and handles and bars. I could wreck the whole thing in a few minutes if I started pushing buttons and pressing bars. But the engineer knows—and he gets the proper results when he pushes the right buttons.

So, when God Almighty stepped into the cab of His locomotive, which we call the cosmos, He was at the controls and He has always pushed the right buttons. Just because there are things in the universe beyond my human explanation does not allow me to accuse God of making a lot of unnecessary truck to clutter up the universe. God made everything for some purpose.

I have mentioned utility in this regard. In the book of Genesis, we find that usefulness was God's first plan. God said, "Let there be light," and He saw that it was good and that it had a purpose. So He divided the light from the darkness, and called the light day and the darkness night.

God did the same thing with the waters and throughout those two chapters of Genesis there is a beautiful exercise in utility—God making an orderly world for a purpose, with everything having a reason for existence.

With God usefulness was first, and so it is with people.

Whenever a pioneering man has gone out to the undeveloped plains to get himself a homestead, a little plot of ground which is to become his home, he does not think about beauty but about utility and usefulness. He knows he must have a log house or some kind of safe dwelling before the blizzards come. You will still find many such plain, often ugly houses scattered throughout the West. It is a place to live, it is home, it is a place to rest when a man is tired. It may be primitive, but it fulfills its purpose.

In the second place, God added decoration. That is the expression that is actually in the Greek root. The word *decorative* is in it. First, He created for utility and purpose and then added decoration and beauty. There probably is a sense in which we could get along without the decoration, but it is a lot better to have it. There is that which is in the mind of God that desires to be pleased—not only satisfied. Order and usefulness and purpose bring satisfaction, but God desired that there should be beauty in His work.

I think it would be a great thing if more human beings discovered the truth that it does not cost any more to have things pleasing and beautiful than it does to have them useful and ugly. We could start out right here in our own city. You start to drive out of the city in almost any direction and you soon wonder if there is anything beautiful left in the world. Smoke stacks and smell and the sprawling apparatus for making gasoline out of crude oil—ugly, ugly, ugly! But, of course, the utility is inherent in our factories and foundaries and refineries. If it were not for that kind of utility, many of you could not have driven to church—useful but not beautiful.

Well, perhaps the day will come in the millennium when we will make things beautiful as well as useful. I still think it does not cost any more to add the beauty and the pleasure and the delight. It costs no more to raise a beautiful daughter than to raise a homely daughter, and a beautiful wife does not eat any more than a homely wife.

You choose two men and give each of them a pot of paint, and one of them will turn out a masterpiece to hang in a gallery, and the other will turn out a horrible insult to the human imagination. All of that with just the same amount of paint and just the same amount of time. One is an artist and the other is a dauber.

Give two architects a free hand, each with a carload of bricks, and one will come up with a monstrosity—like some church buildings I have seen—while the other will add a touch entirely pleasing and satisfying. The costs will be the same—it is just a question of beauty in arrangement.

God could have made a river to go roaring right down to the sea—a plain, straight, ugly-looking channel. It would have fed the fish and done its job. But I think God smiled and made it to meander around under trees and around hills, a stream that catches the blue of the sky and reflects it to those nearby. People are intrigued by the meandering stream and comment, "Isn't it beautiful?" And God says, "Thank you for seeing it. I made you to see it." God is able to make things useful and beautiful. That is what the word *world* means.

Now, you say, what is this—a lecture on art?

No, it is a theological talk on what the word *world* means in the Bible—the created world which is God Almighty's decorated order which He watches and tends.

The other use of this word *world* is that which means mankind—the organized world and society of men and women.

When God reports that Christ was in the world and the world neither recognized nor knew Him, He was not referring to the created clouds and hills and rocks and rivers. He was referring to human society, the world of mankind, and it was this organized world of man that knew Him not.

John testified that God's World, His only begotten Son, became flesh and dwelt among us. What was He doing in our kind of world, in our kind of fallen society?

Before the incarnation, He was the all-permeating Word of God moving creatively in His universe. When Jesus Christ became man, God incarnate in a human body, He did not cease to be the all-permeating Word of God. To this very day, the all-permeating Word still fills the universe and moves among us.

How few men there are who realize His presence, who realize that they have Him to deal with. He is still the Light of the world. It is He that lighteth every man that cometh into the world. After His ascension from Olivet's mountain, He still remains as the all-permeating, vitalizing, life-giving Word operative in the universe.

What is He doing in the universe?

The scriptures tell us that "by him were all things created, that are in heaven, and that are in earth, visible and invisible, whether they be thrones, or dominions, or principalities, or powers: all things were created by him, and for him: and he is before all things (in time), and by him all things consist (or hold together)." The all-permeating Word which is in the world is the adhesive quality of the universe. That is why we do not fall apart. He is, in a very true sense, the mortar and the magnetism that holds all things together.

That is why He is here, for this is not a dead planet that we inhabit. Sin is the only dead thing. This is a living world we inhabit and it is held together by the spiritual presence of the invisible Word. He was in the world and the world was made by Him.

The scriptures continue speaking of Him: "Who being the brightness of his (God's) glory, . . . and upholding all things by the word of his power, when he had by himself purged our sins, sat down on the right hand of the Majesty on high." He is upholding all things by the word of His power.

When a little child looks up into the starry sky at night there may be a natural and childish fear that the sky will fall down. The parents laugh and pat the child on the head and apologize that he is tired—but the child is not as dumb as we might think.

Why doesn't the sky fall down? Why is it that stars and planets do not go tearing apart and ripping off into chaos?

Because there is a Presence that makes all things consist—and it is the Presence of that One who upholdeth all things by the word of His power. This is basically a spiritual explanation, for this universe can only be explained by spiritual and eternal laws. This is why the scientists can never manage to get through to the root of all things and never will, for they deal only with the things that they can see and touch and taste and mix in the experimental test tubes.

The scientist does not know how to deal with this mysterious Presence and Force that holds all things together. He can mix elements and chemicals and note the reactions that take place and then write an article and say, "I did not see God in the formula." But the scientist is only able to come up with dependable and consistent formulas because of God's faithfulness and power in holding all things together.

The scientist announces that a certain star will be in a definite place in the universe after another 2,510 years and twenty minutes! Then he sits back from his computer and boasts, "I have run God out of His world! I can predict where the stars will be in the future."

Oh, what a foolish man! The stars would all grind themselves to powder unless God in His faithfulness continues to keep them in their course and in their systems. He upholds all things by the word of His power.

Again, we read in the scriptures: "Lift up your eyes on high, and behold who hath created these things, that bringeth out their host by number: he calleth them all by names by the greatness of his might, for that he is strong in power; not one faileth."

We lose a good deal of the expression of this passage in our English translation, but it is still one of the most beautiful in the Bible. It is a companion piece to the twenty-third Psalm, dealing with the astronomical host instead of His care for human beings.

The man of God says, "Lift up your eyes on high, and behold who hath created all these things." He is referring to that great display of shining, bright, diamond things that look down upon the country and the city and reflect on the waters of the sea. These stars yonder—who has created these things that bring out their host by number?

Why do they bring out their host?

Because they are like sheep, and this is the figure of a shepherd bringing his sheep out by number and calling them all by name, counting them as they come out and naming every one, and leading them across the green grass of the meadows and beside the still waters.

So, the shepherd-minded poet, Isaiah, saw that the starry hosts above were like a flock of sheep and that God, the great Shepherd, called and they came sailing out through the inter-stellar space as He numbered them and said, "They are all here!" Then He called them by their names, throughout the boundless universe, and because He is strong in power, not one faileth!

I believe that this can be said to be the most majestic and elevated figure of speech in the entire Bible—with no possible exception. We still know so little about the far reaches of the universe, but the astronomers tell us that the very

Milky Way is not a milky way at all—but simply an incredible profusion of stars, billions of light-years away, and yet all moving in their prescribed and orderly directions.

We delight in the fact that it was God who called them all out, who knows their numbers, and He calls them all by name as a shepherd calls his sheep. What a lofty, brain-stretching illustration of what God is doing in His universe, holding all things together in proper courses and orbits.

He is that kind of Creator and God—yet the world knew Him not. That is mankind. He is still in the world, but mankind scoffs in its ignorance of Him, almost completely unaware of His revelation that the Word can be known and honored and loved by the humble human heart.

Now, the Word in His Presence can be known by mankind of the world. I am not conferring salvation upon every man by this statement. I mean to say that an awareness and consciousness of the Presence of God has often been known among men.

May I put it like this?

In the early days of America, when our founding fathers were writing constitutions and drafting laws and making history, many of the men in high places were not believing Christians. As a nation, we have been dreamy-eyed about some of those old boys and have made them out to be Christians when they were not.

I recall that Benjamin Franklin, who often said that he was not a believing Christian, suggested prayer to Almighty God at a time when the young nation was being threatened. The leaders did pray and they got out of the right place.

Now, Franklin was not a Christian, but he believed there was a God operative in the world and he did not deny the awareness of that Presence. Daniel Webster confessed that the profoundest thought he had ever entertained in his life was his "responsibility to a holy God."

Surely, our fathers were not all fundamental Christians and many were not born again, but most of them were men who held a reverent and profound belief in the presence of God in His world. A modern generation considers them old-fashioned and laughs at them, but they drafted far-sighted legislation and a world-renowned code of personal and national ethics and responsibilities that remain to this day.

Standing up for the awareness and consciousness of a Creator God did not save them, but it stamped them in character and manhood as apart from some of the poker-playing, whiskey-drinking rascals who have never given any thought to the idea of God and His Presence in our day. The Word is in the world and the world knows Him not—but it is possible to know.

A Moslem falls down on the ground five times a day in reverence to God in heaven—and a lot of people laugh at him. The Hindu measures himself painfully on the way to the Ganges river to bathe himself—and a lot of people comment, "How foolish can you get?"

But I would rather be a Moslem or a Hindu or a primitive tribesman living in a cootie-infested hut in Africa, kneeling before bones and feathers and mumbling some kind of home-made prayer, than to come into judgment as a self-sufficient American businessman who ruled God out of his life and out of his business and out of his home.

Many an unthinking, secular-minded American would reply: "I'm willing to take my chances!"

What foolish talk from a mortal man!

Men do not have the luxury of taking their chances—either they are saved or they are lost. Surely this is the great curse that lies upon mankind today—men are so wrapped up in their own godless world that they refuse the Light that shines, the Voice that speaks, and the Presence that pervades.

If you can stop this modern, self-sufficient man long

enough to talk, he will assure you that preaching is for the down-and-out bum on Skid Row. He will assure you that he has never robbed a bank, that he is a good husband and a good citizen.

Citizenship is not the final issue with God. Morality and obeying the law are not the final issues with God. The Spirit of God tries to speak to this modern man of the great curse that lies upon his heart and life—he has become so absorbed with money and bank accounts and profit and loss and markets and loans and interest that any thought of God and salvation and eternity has been crowded out. There are dollar signs before his eyes and he would rather close another deal and make a neat profit than to make his way into the kingdom of God.

Many others in our human society are completely hooked on fame and notoriety and public attention. A well-known actress and singer recently told the press about her long career and the fame and fortune which have come to her, and she summed it all up in these words: "Fate made me what I am!"

After an entire life absorbed in a godless world and society, no better answer than some kind of esoteric, weird fate. She has lived only for the kind of fame and notice that men can give, and she would rather have her name on the marquee of a theater than to have it eternally inscribed in the Lamb's Book of Life. The Voice has been here with us, but she has never heeded it. The Light is here, but she has never seen it. The Presence is in our world, but she cannot feel it.

Money and profits, fame and fortune—and with millions of others it is a complete addiction to pleasure. Flesh contacts, nerve endings, sensuous delight, carnal joy—anything to keep humans from sensing that there is a Presence, the Way, the Truth and the Light.

Brethren, do not charge me with acting like a mystic.

Instead, hear again these words of scripture: "In him

was life; and the life was the light of men. And the light shineth in darkness; and the darkness comprehended it not." And "in the beginning was the Word," and the Word "was in the world."

Now, there is the Word—and He is the Voice and He is the Light.

And the Word "was in the world"—there is His Presence. This is not poetry. This is the truth of God. And because our generation does not recognize the Voice and does not perceive the Light and has no sense of the Presence, we have become a profane generation. We dote on things—secular things—until we mistakenly assume that there is nothing in the universe but material and physical values. The profane man has come to the conclusion that he alone is important in this universe—thus he becomes his own god.

It is sad but true that a great and eternal woe awaits the profane and completely secular man whose only religion is in the thought that he probably is not as bad as some other man. I think that there is an Old Testament portion in the book of Job that fits modern, profane man very well: "Woe is me, that I was ever born, that my mother ever conceived me. Let the stars of the twilight of that night be as darkness. Oh, that I might have been carried from my mother's knees to the grave, where the wicked cease from troubling and the toil-worn are dressed."

I am thinking actually of men who give lip service to the church and some mental assent to religion, but they have forgotten that they were created, that they have a responsibility to God, and they have ignored Jesus Christ—His Presence, His Voice, His Light.

Actually, you can be too bright and too educated and too sophisticated, and thus fail to hear and to heed God's entreaty. But you cannot be too simple!

I was an ignorant 17-year-old boy when I first heard preaching on the street, and I was moved to wander into a church where I heard a man quoting a text: "Come unto me, all ye that labour and are heavy laden, and I will give you rest. Take my yoke upon you, and learn of me; for I am meek and lowly in heart: and ye shall find rest unto your souls."

Actually, I was little better than a pagan, but with only that kind of skimpy biblical background, I became greatly disturbed, for I began to feel and sense and acknowledge God's gracious Presence. I heard His Voice—ever so faintly. I discerned that there was a Light—ever so dimly.

I was still lost, but thank God, I was getting closer. The Lord Jesus knows that there are such among us today, of whom He says: "Ye are not far from the kingdom of God."

Once again, walking on the street, I stopped to hear a man preaching at a corner, and he said to those listening: "If you do not know how to pray, go home and get down and ask, 'God, have mercy on me, a sinner.'"

That is exactly what I did, and in spite of the dispensational teachers who tell me that I used the wrong text, I got into my Father's house. I got my feet under my Father's table. I got hold of a big spoon and I have been enjoying my Father's spiritual blessings ever since.

Actually, I have paid no attention to those brethren pounding on the window outside, shouting at me and beckoning to me, "Come on out of there, boy. You got in by the wrong door!"

Dispensations or not, God has promised to forgive and satisfy anyone who is hungry enough and concerned enough and anxious enough to cry out, "Lord, save me!"

When Peter was starting to sink under those waters of Galilee, he had no time to consult the margin of someone's Bible to find out how he should pray. He just prayed out of his heart and out of his desperation, "Lord, save me!" And his Lord answered.

Brethren, why don't we just let our hearts do the praying? If a man will just get his heart down on its knees, he will find that there is an awful lot that he does not need to know to receive Jesus Christ!

He is here now. "The Word became flesh and dwelt among us." He went away in His human body, but He is still with us—the everlasting, all-permeating Word—still with us to save! He only waits for a childlike prayer from a humble and needy heart—"Oh, Lamb of God, I come, I come!"

Excerpts from
God Tells the Man Who Cares

Honesty in Prayer
Pragmatism Goes to Church
Faith Without Expectation Is Dead
A Christian and His Money

38

Honesty in Prayer

The saintly David M'Intyre, in his radiant little book, *The Hidden Life of Prayer*, deals frankly, if briefly, with a vital element of true prayer which in our artificial age is likely to be overlooked.

We mean just plain honesty.

"Honest dealing becomes us," says M'Intyre, "when we kneel in His pure presence."

"In our address to God," he continues, "we like to speak of Him as we think we ought to speak, and there are times when our words far outrun our feelings. But it is best that we should be perfectly frank before Him. He will allow us to say anything we will, so long as it is to Himself. 'I will say unto God, my rock,' exlaims the psalmist, 'why hast thou forgotten me?' If he had said, 'Lord, thou canst not forget. Thou hast graven my name on the palms of thy hands,' he would have spoken more worthily, but less truly.

"On one occasion Jeremiah failed to interpret God aright. He cried as if in anger, 'O Lord, thou hast deceived me, and I was deceived.' These are terrible words to utter before Him who is changeless truth. But the prophet spoke as he felt, and the Lord not only pardoned him, but met him and blessed him there."

So far M'Intyre. Another spiritual writer of unusual penetration has advised frankness in prayer even to a degree that might appear to be downright rudeness. When you come to prayer, he says, and find that you have no taste for it, tell God so without mincing words. If God and spiritual things bore you, admit it frankly. This advice will shock some squeamish saints, but it is altogether sound nevertheless. God loves the guileless soul even when in his ignorance he is actually guilty of rashness in prayer. The Lord can soon cure his ignorance, but for insincerity no cure is known.

The basic artificiality of civilized human beings is hard to shake off. It gets into our very blood and conditions our thoughts, attitudes and relationships much more seriously than we imagine. A book on human relations has appeared within recent years whose underlying philosophy is deception and whose recommended technique is a skillful use of flattery to gain desired ends. It has had an unbelievably wide sale, actually running into the millions. Of course its popularity may be explained by the fact that it said what people wanted to hear.

The desire to make a good impression has become one of the most powerful of all the factors determining human conduct. That gracious (and scriptural) social lubricant called courtesy has in our times degenerated into a completely false and phony etiquette that hides the true man under a shimmery surface as thin as the oil slick on a quiet pond. The only time some persons expose their real self is when they get mad.

With this perverted courtesy determining almost everything men say and do in human society it is not surprising that it should be hard to be completely honest in our relations with God. It carries over as a kind of mental reflex and is present without our being aware of it. Nevertheless, it is extremely hateful to God. Christ detested it and condemned it without mercy when He found it among the Pharisees. The artless little child is still the divine model for all of us. Prayer will increase in power and reality as we repudiate all pretense and learn to be utterly honest before God as well as before men.

A great Christian of the past broke out all at once into a place of such radiance and victory as to excite wonder among his friends. Someone asked him what had happened to him. He replied simply that his new life of power began one day when he entered the presence of God and took a solemn vow never again to say anything to God in prayer that he did not mean. His transformation began with that vow and continued as he kept it.

We can learn something there if we will.

39

Pragmatism Goes to Church

It is not by accident that the philosophy of pragmatism around the turn of the century achieved such wide popularity in the United States. The American temperament was perfect for it, and still is.

Pragmatism has a number of facets and can mean various things to various people, but basically it is the doctrine of the utility of truth. For the pragmatist there are no absolutes; nothing is absolutely good or absolutely true. Truth and morality float on a sea of human experience. If an exhausted swimmer can lay hold of a belief or an ethic, well and good; it may keep him afloat till he can get to shore; then it only encumbers him, so he tosses it away. He feels no responsibility to cherish truth for its own sake. It is there to serve him; he has no obligation to serve it.

Truth is to use. Whatever is useful is true for the user, though for someone else it may not be useful, so not true. The truth of any idea is its ability to produce desirable results. If it can show no such results it is false. That is pragmatism stripped of its jargon.

Now, since practicality is a marked characteristic of the American people they naturally lean strongly toward the philosophy of utility. Whatever will get things done immediately with a maximum of efficiency and a minimum of undesirable side effects must be good. The proof is that it succeeds; no one wants to argue with success.

It is useless to plead for the human soul, to insist that what a man can do is less important than what he is. When there are wars to be won, forests to be cleared, rivers to be harnessed, factories to be built, planets to be visited, the quieter claims of the human spirit are likely to go unregarded. The spectacular drama of successful deeds leaves the beholder breathless. Deeds you can see. Factories, cities, highways, rockets are there in plain sight, and they got there by the practical application of means to ends. So who cares about ideals and character and morals? These things are for poets, nice old ladies and philosophers. Let's get on with the job.

Now all this has been said, and said better, a few dozen times before, and I would not waste space on it here except that this philosophy of pragmatism has had and is having a powerful influence upon Christianity in the middle years of this century. And whatever touches the faith of Christ immediately becomes a matter of interest to me and, I hope, to my readers also.

The nervous compulsion to get things done is found everywhere among us. We are affected by a kind of religious tic, a deep inner necessity to accomplish something that can be seen and photographed and evaluated in terms of size, numbers, speed and distance. We travel a prodigious number of miles, talk to unbelievably large crowds, publish an astonishing amount of religious literature, collect huge sums of money, build vast numbers of churches and amass staggering debts for our children to pay. Christian leaders compete with each other in the field of impressive statistics, and in so doing often acquire peptic ulcers, have nervous breaks or die of heart attacks while still relatively young.

Right here is where the pragmatic philosophy comes into its own. It asks no embarrassing questions about the wisdom of what we are doing or even about the morality of it. It accepts our chosen ends as right and good and casts about for efficient means and ways to get them accomplished. When it discovers something that works it soon finds a text to justify it, "consecrates" it to the Lord and plunges ahead. Next a magazine article is written about it, then a book, and finally the inventor is granted an honorary degree. After that any question about the scripturalness of things or even the moral validity of them is completely swept away. You cannot argue with success. The method works; *ergo*, it must be good.

The weakness of all this is its tragic shortsightedness. It never takes the long view of religious activity, indeed it dare not do so, but goes cheerfully on believing that because it works it is both good and true. It is satisfied with present success and shakes off any suggestion that its works may go up in smoke in the day of Christ.

As one fairly familiar with the contemporary religious scene, I say without hesitation that a part, a very large part, of the activities carried on today in evangelical circles are not only influenced by pragmatism but almost completely controlled by it. Religious methodology is geared to it; it appears large in our youth meetings; magazines and books constantly glorify it; conventions are dominated by it; and the whole religious atmosphere is alive with it.

What shall we do to break its power over us? The answer is simple. *We must acknowledge the right of Jesus Christ to control the activities of His church.* The New Testament contains full instructions, not only about what we are to believe but what we are to do and how we are to go about doing it. *Any deviation from those instructions is a denial of the Lordship of Christ.*

I say the answer is simple, but it is not easy for it requires that we obey God rather than man, and that always brings down the wrath of the religious majority. It is not a question of knowing what to do; we can easily learn that from the Scriptures. It is a question of whether or not we have the courage to do it.

40

Faith Without Expectation
Is Dead

Expectation and faith, though alike, are not identical. An instructed Christian will not confuse the two.

True faith is never found alone; it is always accompanied by expectation. The man who believes the promises of God expects to see them fulfilled. Where there is no expectation there is no faith.

It is, however, quite possible for expectation to be present where no faith is. The mind is quite capable of mistaking strong desire for faith. Indeed faith, as commonly understood, is little more than desire compounded with cheerful optimism. Certain writers make a comfortable living promoting that kind of so-called faith which is supposed to create the "positive" as opposed to the negative mind. Their effusions are dear to the hearts of those in the population who are afflicted with a psychological compulsion to believe, and who manage to live with facts only by the simple expedient of ignoring them.

Real faith is not the stuff dreams are made of; rather it is tough, practical and altogether realistic. Faith sees the invisible but it does not see the nonexistent. Faith engages God, the one great Reality, who gave and gives existence to all things. God's promises conform to reality, and whoever trusts them enters a world not of fiction but of fact.

In common experience we arrive at truth by observation. Whatever can be verified by experiment is accepted as true.

Men believe the report of their senses. If it walks like a duck, looks like a duck and quacks like a duck it is probably a duck. And if its eggs hatch into little ducks the test is about complete. Probability gives way to certainty; it is a duck. This is a valid way to deal with our environment. No one dare complain about it for everyone does it. It is the way we manage to get on in this world.

But faith introduces another and radically different element into our lives. "By faith we know" is the word that lifts our knowing onto a higher level. Faith engages facts that have been revealed from heaven and by their nature they do not respond to scientific tests. The Christian knows a thing to be true, not because he has verified it in experience but because God has said it. His expectations spring from his confidence in the character of God.

Expectation has always been present in the church in the times of her greatest power. When she believed, she expected, and her Lord never disappointed her. "And blessed is she that believed: for there shall be a performance of those things which were told her from the Lord."

Every great movement of God in history, every unusual advance in the church, every revival, has been preceded by a sense of keen anticipation. Expectation accompanied the operations of the Spirit always. His bestowals hardly surprised His people because they were gazing expectantly toward the risen Lord and looking confidently for His word to be fulfilled. His blessings accorded with their expectations.

One characteristic that marks the average church today is lack of anticipation. Christians when they meet do not expect anything unusual to happen; consequently only the usual happens, and that usual is as predictable as the setting of the sun. A psychology of nonexpectation prevades the assembly, a mood of quiet ennui which the minister by various means tries to dispel, the means depending upon the cultural level of the congregation and particularly of the minister.

One will resort to humor, another will latch on to some topic currently dividing the public, such as fluoridation, capital punishment or Sunday sports. Another who may have a modest opinion of his gifts as a humorist and who is not sure which side of a controversy he may safely support will seek to arouse expectation by outlining enthusiastically the shape of things to come: the Men's Banquet to be held at the Chicken-in-a-Basket Tea Room next Thursday evening; or the picnic with its thrilling game to be played between the Married Men and the Single Men, the outcome of which the jocular minister coyly refuses to predict; or the coming premier of the new religious film, full of sex, violence and false philosophy but candied over with vapid moralizings and gentle suggestions that the enraptured viewers should be born again.

The activities of the saints are thus laid out for them by those who are supposed to know what they need better than they do. And this planned play is made acceptable to the more pious-minded by tagging on a few words of devotion at the close. This is called "fellowship," though it bears scant resemblance to the activities of those Christians to which the word was first applied.

Christian expectation in the average church follows the program, not the promises. Prevailing spiritual conditions, however low, are accepted as inevitable. What will be is what has been. The weary slaves of the dull routine find it impossible to hope for anything better.

We need today a fresh spirit of anticipation that springs out of the promises of God. We must declare war on the mood of nonexpectation, and come together with childlike faith. Only then can we know again the beauty and wonder of the Lord's presence among us.

41

A Christian and His Money

The whole question of the believer and his money is so involved and so intimate that one hesitates to approach a consideration of it. Yet it is of such grave importance that one who desires to qualify as a good servant of Christ dare not avoid it lest he be found wanting in the day of reckoning. Someone should tackle the problem in the light of Scripture. God's people will have reason to thank the man who has the courage to deal with it.

Four considerations should govern our Christian giving. They are: (1) That we give systematically; (2) that we give from a right motive; (3) that we give enough in proportion to what we possess, and (4) that we give to the right place or places.

First, we should see to it that we give of our substance to the Lord with regularity. It is so very easy to fall into the habit of forgetting to do this. We tell ourselves that we are not able to give at the moment, but that when we are better fixed financially we shall catch up on our giving. Or we assure ourselves that while we do not give systematically we no doubt give far beyond our tenth, if the truth were known. These are sure ways to deceive ourselves. Spotty, unsystematic giving has a way of appearing far greater than it is. We would likely be quite shocked if we took the trouble to find out just how little we really give that way.

Then we must give from a right motive. Money paid to a

church or missionary society may be for the giver money wasted unless he first makes sure that his heart is in his gift. Gifts that do not carry the heart with them may do the receiver some good, but it is certain that they will bring the giver no reward. "Though I bestow all my goods to feed the poor . . . and have not charity (love), it profiteth me nothing."

Then it is also important that we give enough in proportion to what we possess. The story of the widow and her two mites makes this very clear. The widow gave out of her "poverty," and though her gift was small it was in the sight of God a far greater treasure than all the huge sums donated by the rich "out of their abundance." This is a solemn warning and we shall do well to heed it.

We humans judge "after the sight of our eyes" and so are prone to make a great deal over a large donation and pass over the small ones without comment. By so doing we are letting ourselves in for a fearful shock in the day of Christ. The safest rule to appraise our giving and determine our expectations in the day of rewards is this: Remember, *my giving will be rewarded not by how much I gave but by how much I had left.* Ministers are sometimes tempted to shy away from such doctrine as this lest they offend the important givers in their congregation. But it is better to offend men than to grieve the blessed Spirit of God which dwells in the church. No man ever yet killed a true church by withdrawing his gifts from it because of a personal pique. The Church of the Firstborn is not dependent upon the patronage of men. No man has ever been able really to harm a church by boycotting it financially. The moment we admit that we fear the displeasure of the carnal givers in our congregations we admit also that our congregations are not of heaven but of the earth. A heavenly church will enjoy a heavenly and supernatural prosperity. She cannot be starved out. The Lord will supply her needs.

That we place our gifts intelligently is also of vital importance if we would please our Heavenly Father and save those gifts from the fate of "wood, hay and stubble" at the coming of our Lord.

The matter of where to give is a large one, and one that we had all better settle while we can. Careless, unintelligent and prejudiced giving is wasting millions of consecrated dollars among evangelical Christians. Many believers toss their gifts around as if they did not expect to give an account of them to the Lord. They have not found the mind of the Lord on the question of their own giving, so they become the prey of anyone who happens along with an interesting story. In this way innumerable religious rackets are enabled to flourish which should never receive one cent from serious-minded and God-honoring people.

Now, we are quite aware that the reply to the above could be a polite request that we stay in our own back yard and let people put their own money where they please; after all it is theirs, and what they do with it is their own affair. But it is not that simple. If we must give account of every idle word, surely we must also give account of every idle dollar. Spotty, prayerless and whimsical giving will come under the just scrutiny of God in the day when He judges every work of men. We can do something about this whole thing now. Very soon it will be too late.

Denominations Can Backslide, Too

42

Denominations
Can Backslide Too!

Oh, that we would have a naked intent to know Jesus Christ! It means putting the world and things and people beneath our feet, opening our hearts to only one lover—the Son of God Himself!

Our problems of spiritual coldness and apathy in the churches would quickly disappear if Christian believers generally would confess their great need for rediscovering the loveliness of Jesus Christ, their Saviour.

I have good scriptural ground for constantly emphasizing my deep concern that Christians should again begin to love our Lord Jesus with an intensity of love and desire such as our fathers knew.

What is basically wrong with us when we start to backslide as individuals or as churches and denominations?

Jesus Himself gave us a plain answer when He said, "You have left your first degree of love!" He was not speaking of first love as first in consecutive order, but of the degree of our first love for Him.

These words of Jesus reflect one of our great weaknesses in the Christian churches of our day. The fact that we are not going on to know Christ in rich intimacy of acquaintance and fellowship is apparent—but why are we not even willing to talk about it? We are not hearing anything about spiritual desire and yearning and the loveliness of our Saviour which would break down all barriers if we would move into communion with Him. This appeal is not getting into our books. You don't hear it in radio messages. It is not being preached in our churches.

Can it be that we do not believe that Jesus Christ is capable of a growing and increasing intimacy of fellowship with those who are His own? To become acquainted with God is one thing, but to go on in commitment and to experience God in intensity and richness of acquaintance is something more. The Apostle Paul knew this in his yearning as he said, "I want to know Him in that depth and rich intensity of experience!" Of the many compelling reasons why we ought to know our Saviour better than we do certainly the first is that He is a person, Jesus Christ. We all agree that He is a person, that He is the Eternal Son, but have we gone on to adore Him because He is the source and fountain of everything that you and I are created to enjoy?

He is the fountain of all truth, but He is more—He is truth itself. He is the source and strength of all beauty, but He is more—He is beauty itself. He is the fountain of all wisdom, but He is more—He is wisdom itself. In Him are all the treasures of wisdom and knowledge hidden away!

Jesus Christ our Saviour is the fountain of all grace. He is the fountain and source of all life, but He is more than that. He could say, "I *AM* the life!" He is the fountain of love, but again, He is far more than that—He is love!

He is resurrection and He is immortality and as one of the adoring song writers said, He is the "brightness of the Father's glory, sunshine of the Father's face."

In another hymn, "Fairest Lord Jesus," there are at least two verses that are not always included, which tell us in candor and realism that when everything else has perished and vanished, we will find it is Jesus alone who abides for aye. One verse says, "Earth's fairest beauty, heaven's brightest splendor, in Jesus Christ unfolded see; all that here shineth quickly declineth before His spotless purity."

There is excitement in true love, and I think that we Christians who love our Saviour ought to be more excited about Who He is and What He is!

A friend of mine has been quite irked because I cannot get excited and steamed up about earthly things. I just cannot stand and strike an attitude of awe when a friend drives up with one of the classy new automobiles. I hear people describing the magnificent new houses that they are building, and they have excitement in their voices. But the Word of God forces me to remember that when you have seen the house or the city that hath foundations and whose builder and maker is God, you cannot really ever get excited again about any house ever built by any man in this world.

It has been said that Abraham could never build a permanent house for himself after he had seen the city whose builder and maker was God. I know I have made up my mind about that city—and I would be willing to live in a tent here because I have some idea about my future home up there. I am convinced that it will be beautiful and satisfying beyond anything I can know down here. It is a tragedy if we forget that "earth's fairest beauty and heaven's brightest splendor are all unfolded in Jesus Christ, and all that here shineth quickly declineth before His spotless purity."

The man who wrote those words, breathed them from his soul, must have been one of God's special kind of Christians. He must have known Jesus Christ intimately day by day. He probably knew all about the cost of knowing the Saviour in this way.

But people are not willing to pay that price, and that is why so many Christians must be described as "common." Most Christians talk piously about the cost of Christianity in terms of the unclean, injurious and grossly sinful things they have "surrendered." But if they never get beyond that they are still common Christians. They talk about having given up the bad things, but the Apostle Paul said that for

Christ's sake he surrendered the good things as well as the bad.

"What things were gain to me I count but loss," he said. He meant things to which he still had a legal and moral right, things about which he could have said, "These are mine and Christianity is not going to take them from me!"

"I yield them all, I give them all because I have found That which is so much better," he wrote. He had found "That" which was with the Father, Jesus Christ, the fountain from Whom flows all wisdom and beauty and truth and immortality!

Paul knew something that many Christians still have not learned—that the human heart is idolatrous and will worship anything it can possess. Therein lies the danger of the "good" things. We have surrendered evil things, bad things, but we hold on to the good things and these we are prone to worship. Whatever we refuse to surrender and count but loss we will ultimately worship. It may be something good, but it gets between you and God—whether it be property or family or reputation or security or your life itself.

Jesus warned us about our selfishness in grasping and hanging on to our own lives. He taught that if we make our life on earth so important and so all-possessing that we cannot surrender it gladly to Him, we will lose it at last. He taught that plainly, and He also warned us about trusting earthly security rather than putting our complete confidence in God.

We all want a guarantee of security, but we didn't get that idea from the Apostle Paul. He was hardly ever secure as far as the things of this life were concerned. He said he died daily. He was always in difficulty, whether with the governments of this world or with the stormy elements on the sea.

Brethren, we want security in this life and eternal security in the world above! I think that is a kind of definition of our modern-day Christian fundamentalism. But Paul said, "I have been captured by Jesus Christ so I disavow and disown everything."

Now there were certain things that God let Paul have. He let him have a book or two. He let him have a garment, a cloak. In one instance, He let him have his own hired house for two years. But the example Paul gave us was the fact that any "things" which God allowed him to have never touched him at heart, at the point of possession.

Any of our external treasures which really bind us at heart will become a curse. Paul said, "I give them up that I might know Him." He never allowed things to become important enough to mar his relationship with God.

The example and admonitions of Paul cause me to call into question some of the teachings in our current Christian circles that Christ is something "added on"—that by ourselves we can have a rather jolly earthly life, but we also need Jesus to save us from hell and to get us into the mansions on the other side!

Now, that is not New Testament teaching and certainly not the way in which Paul looked at things in this world. Paul said that he found Jesus Christ so infinitely attractive that he was forced to throw out every set of values established on earth.

Paul was a learned man, an intellectual educated at the feet of Gamaliel. We would have honored him as a Ph.D. But Paul said, "That is all dross." His expression actually meant: "It is a kind of garbage."

Paul spoke of his birth and of his register and standing among the fathers of his religious heritage and then testified that "for the sake of Jesus Christ, I count it nothing at all—I put it under my feet."

That ought to say something to us who have so many things about which we are proud. Some of us boast about our national and cultural forebears until we actually become carnal about it. We are proud of things and proud of what we can do. But Paul said, "Everything about which I could be proud as a man I count but loss for the sake of Jesus Christ."

So Paul gives us the proper motives for loving and following the Saviour and for giving up the things that would hold us back. Modern Christianity has a lot to learn from Paul in this area of motives. Because of the nature of our times, some are insisting: "America, you had better turn to God or that final bomb will get you!" Another voice of alarm warns: "America, you had better stop drinking and gambling or you will go down like Rome!"

Our old teacher-friend, *The Cloud of Unknowing*, gives us some light on proper motives in relationship to the nature of God Himself. "God is a jealous lover and He suffereth no rival," this saint wrote more than 600 years ago. "God cannot work in our wills unless He can possess our wills for Himself."

Now brethren, this is one of our greatest faults in our Christian lives. We are allowing too many rivals of God. We actually have too many gods. We have too many irons in the fire. We have too much theology that we don't understand. We have too much churchly institutionalism. We have too much religion. Actually, I guess we just have too much of too much!

God is not in our beings by Himself! He cannot do His will in us and through us because we refuse to put away the rivals. When Jesus Christ has cleansed everything from the temple and dwells there alone, He will work!

God wants to do His work hidden and unseen within the human breast. Have you ever been deep down in a mine in the earth? They are mining out coal or gold or diamonds, but anyone flying or walking or traveling overhead may have no idea of what is going on in the depths of that hill. They would never know that deep within the earth there is an intelligent force at work bringing out jewels. That is what God does deep within us—and He works hidden and unseen.

But in our day we must be dramatic about everything. We don't want God to work unless He can make a theatrical production of it. We want Him to come dressed in costumes with a beard and with a staff. We want Him to play a part according to our ideas. Some of us even demand that He provide a colorful setting and fireworks as well!

That is how we want it, but God says, "No, no, no! You children of Adam, you children of carnality and lust, you who love a fair showing of flesh, you who have wrong ideas about my Son, I cannot do my work according to your prescription. I cannot do my work in you!"

How can God do His work in people who seem to think that Christianity is just another way of getting things from God?

I hear people testify that they give their tithe because God makes their nine-tenths go farther than the ten-tenths. That is not spirituality: that is just plain business. I insist that it is a dangerous thing to associate the working of God with our prosperity and success down here. I cannot promise that if you will follow the Lord you will soon experience financial prosperity, because that is not what He promised His disciples. Down through the years, following the Lord has meant that we count all things but loss for the excellency of the knowledge of Christ.

"And don't some Christians prosper?" you ask.

We have many examples of Christian men whom God has been able to trust with unusual prosperity and as they continue to follow the Lord, they give most of it back to Him. But they haven't made Christianity just a technique of getting things.

I hear people testify about their search for the deeper Christian life and it sounds as though they would like to be able to get it in pill form. It seems that it would have been much more convenient for them if God had arranged religion so they could take it like a pill with a glass of water. They buy books, hoping to get their religion by prescription. But there isn't any such thing. There is a cross. There is a gallows. There is a man with bleeding stripes on his back. There is an apostle with no property, with a tradition of loneliness and weariness and rejection and glory—but there are no pills!

There are a thousand ways in which we try to use the Lord. What about that young fellow studying for the ministry, studying until his eyesight begins to fail, but he wants to use Jesus Christ to make him a famous preacher. They will ordain him, and he will get the title of Reverend and if he writes a book, they will make him a Doctor. But if he has been using Jesus Christ, he is just a common huckster buying and selling and getting gain, and the Lord would drive him out of the temple along with the rest.

Then there are some among us these days who have to depend upon truckloads of gadgets to get their religion going, and I am tempted to ask: What will they do when they don't have the help of the trappings and gadgets? The truck can't come along where they are going!

I heard a man boasting on his radio program about the equipment they were going to bring in from Pennsylvania and Ohio so they could better serve the Lord. I don't know of any fancy kind of equipment which will brighten your testimony or your service for God.

I think of the dear old camp meeting ladies who used to say, "This is my harp of ten strings, and I praise the Lord!" I can see in my mind now those wrinkled hands with brown spots, but as they clapped those wrinkled, aging hands how their faces would shine! And their harp? Just those hands as they clapped and sang praises to God.

Who needs a bushel basket full of clap-trap in order to serve the Lord? You can worship God anywhere if you will let Him work in your being and suffer no rival. You may be still with arthritis so that you can't even get on your knees to pray, but you can look up in your heart, for prayer isn't a matter of getting on your knees. Prayer is the elevation of the heart to God and that is all a man needs to praise, to pray and to worship.

Now here is a strange thing. If you talk about mysticism in our day, every fundamentalist throws his hands high in the air with disgust to let you know that he considers the mystics dreamers, those who believe in the emotion and feeling. But all of those old saints and the fathers of whom I have read taught that you must believe God by a naked, cold intent of your will and then the other things follow along.

A naked intent unto God—those old saints were practical men. They have exhorted us to press on in faith whether we feel like it or not. They have exhorted us to pray—when we feel like it and when we don't. They never taught that we would always be lifted emotionally to the heights. They knew that there are times when your spiritual progress must be by a naked intent unto God.

Oh that we would have this naked intent to know God, to know Jesus Christ! To be able to put the world and things and people beneath our feet and to open our hearts to only one lover, and that the Son of God Himself!

Oh for the proper balance in all of our relationships! Husband and wife, father and son, mother and daughter, business man and partner, taxpayer and citizen—all of these in their proper place; but in the deep of the heart having only the One lover, He who suffers no rival.

Why has God insisted that it should be this way?

Because it is His intention that our understanding and our reason should be broken down and that our whole case should be thrown back on God. Many have known the time of darkness and oppression as they sought to go on with God and to be filled with His fullness. You believed God and you trusted Christ. Whether you felt like it or not, you went on and you believed and you obeyed. You prayed whether you felt like it or not. You straightened things out and you got adjusted in your relationships at home and in business. You quit the wrong things, the things that had been hindering you, whether you felt like it or not. This is faith—a naked intent unto God, and I must tell you this: out of our darkness and out of our stony grief, God will raise a Bethel. Out of the tomb, He will lift you into the sky. Out of darkness, He will lift you into the light!

This is what it means to love Jesus, to know Him just for Himself. How I pray that we may again recapture in our day the glory that men may have known of the beauty of Jesus.

In *The Cloud of Unknowing,* the old saint wrote that because God is a jealous lover, He wants us to be unwilling to think on anything but God Himself.

Now, this was the message of Dr. A. B. Simpson. He shocked and blessed a generation because of his central message: "Jesus—Himself!"

Dr. Simpson was asked to go to England to preach in a Bible conference. He discovered that he was to preach the third of three messages on sanctification—and that is a bad spot to be in. The first fellow said in his sermon that the way to be holy and victorious in the Christian life is to suppress "the old man." His was the position of sanctification by suppression. The second man got up and took the position of eradication, deliverance from the old carnal life by eradication. "Get rid of the old man, pull him up, turn up the roots in the sun to die!"

Doctor Simpson had to get in between there and he took just one word for his text: "Himself." Then he gave his testimony of efforts and struggles to get the victory. He said, "Sometimes I would think I had gotten it, and then I would lose it. What a blessedness when I came to the knowledge that I had been looking in the wrong place, when I found that victory, sanctification, deliverance, purity, holiness—all must be found in Jesus Christ Himself, not in some formula. When I claimed Jesus just for Himself, it became easy and the glory came to my life."

Out of that knowledge and out of that blessing, Dr.

Simpson wrote his famous hymn, "Once it was the blessing, now it is the Lord. Once His gift I wanted, now Himself alone."

This is the basic teaching of the deeper Christian life. It is the willingness to let Jesus Christ Himself be glorified in us and through us. It is the willingness to quit trying to use the Lord for our ends and to let Him work in us for His glory.

That is the kind of revival I am interested in and the only kind—the kind of spiritual reviving and renewing that will cause people to tremble with rapture in the presence of the Lord Jesus Christ.

"Once it was the blessing—now it is the Lord!"

Acceptable Worship

43

Acceptable Worship

God wants us to worship Him. He doesn't need us, for He couldn't be a self-sufficient God and need anything or anybody, but He wants us. When Adam sinned it was not he who cried "God, where art Thou?" It was God who cried "Adam, where art thou?"

Paul, in writing to the Thessalonians, referred to the time when Christ shall come to be glorified in the saints and admired by all them that believe He wants to be glorified. Those are a few proof texts in addition to the one I have read from the Psalms, but more convincing than any proof text is the full import and drift of the Scriptures. The whole substance of the Bible teaches that God wants us to worship Him.

Now, there are good, sound , theological and philosophical reasons for this. But while God wants us to worship Him we cannot worship Him just any way we will. The One who made us to worship Him has decreed how we shall worship Him. He accepts only the worship which He Himself has decreed.

I want to speak of some kinds of worship that God has ruled out. There's no use trying to be nice about it. The kingdom of God has suffered a great deal of harm from fighters—men who would rather fight than pray; but the kingdom of God has also been done great harm by men who would rather be nice than right. I believe that God wants us to be right, though He wants us to be right lovingly.

The first false worship is Cain worship, which is worship without atonement. This kind of worship rests upon three basic errors. One is the error that assumes God to be different from what He is. He who seeks to worship a God he does not know comes without having first been cleansed by the coals from off the altar. But this kind of worship will not be accepted by God.

The second error is that man assumes he occupies a relation to God which he does not occupy. The man who worships without Christ and without the blood of the Lamb and without forgiveness and without cleansing is assuming too much. He is mistaking error for truth, and spiritual tragedy is the result.

The third error is that sin is made less serious than it is in fact. The psychologists and psychiatrists and sociologists and that gang of left-wingers that have come in over the past years have taken the terror out of sin. To worship God acceptably we must be freed from sin. Cain worship is worship out of an unregenerate heart.

And then there is Samaritan worship. It is heretical worship in the correct meaning of the word "heretical." Heresy is picking out what you want to believe and rejecting, or at least ignoring, the rest. This the Samaritans did. They worshiped Jehovah but they didn't worship Jerusalem; they worshiped at Samaria. The history of the Samaritans shows that there were some Jews among them and that they had Jewish theology. But they had their Jewish theology all mixed up with pagan theology, and it was neither fish nor fowl but an unholy mixture of both. That is Samaritan worship, and our Lord said, "Ye worship ye know not what."

Then there is nature worship. That is the worship of the natural man, only on a very poetic and philosophical level. It is an appreciation for the poetry of religion. It's a high enjoyment of the contemplation of the sublime. When I was a young fellow and didn't know any better I studied, more or less for fun, the old-fashioned and now thoroughly repudiated doctrine of phrenology. It says that the shape of your head tells what you are. There are certain bumps on your head that reveal your personality. If you have a bump here just above your forehead, that's the bump of sublimity. You love the sublime.

Such are the poets; they like to look at trees and write sonnets. Well, there's a good deal of religion and supposed worship that is no higher than that. It's simply the enjoyment of nature. People may mistake the rapt feeling they have in the presence of trees and rivers for worship. Ralph Waldo Emerson said that he had at times—on a moonlit night walking across a meadow after a rain and smelling the freshness of the ground and seeing the broken clouds with the moon struggling through—he said he had often been glad to the point of fear. Yet Emerson was not a regenerated man. He did not claim to be.

I want to warn you against the religion that is no more than love, music and poetry. I happen to be somewhat of a fan of good music. I think Beethoven's nine symphonies constitute the greatest body of music ever composed by mortal man. Yet I realize I'm listening to music; I'm not worshiping God necessarily. There's a difference between beautiful sounds beautifully put together and worship. Worship is another matter.

Now, I'm very much concerned that we realize that the worship I'm talking about has a sharp theological definition, that there must be truth in it, that it must lie within the confines of eternal truth or it is rejected.

God is Spirit and they that worship Him must worship Him in Spirit and in truth. Only the Holy Spirit can enable a fallen man to worship God acceptably. As far as that's concerned, only the Holy Spirit can pray acceptably; only the Holy Spirit can do anything acceptably. My brethren, I don't know your position about the gifts of the Spirit, but I believe that all the gifts of the Spirit not only ought to be but have been present in His Church all down the centuries. The Spirit's gifts to the Church are the organs through which the Holy Spirit works, and He cannot work through His Church without the organs being present. You cannot account for Augustine and Chrysostom and Luther and Charnock and Wesley and Finney except they were men gifted by the Holy Ghost.

I believe that the Holy Spirit distributes His gifts severally as He will to the Church and that they are in the Church and have been in the Church all along. Otherwise the Church would have died the day that everybody who had been in the upper chamber died. The Church has been propagated by the Holy Spirit, so we can only worship in the Spirit, we can only pray in the Spirit, and we can only preach effectively in the Spirit, and what we do must be done by the power of the Spirit. I believe that the gifts are in the Body of Christ and they that worship God must worship Him in the Spirit.

But also we must worship Him in truth. Now the worshiper must submit to truth. I can't worship God acceptably unless I have accepted what God has said about five things. Before my worship is accepted I must accept what God has said about Himself. We must never edit God. We must never, never, apologize for God. No man has any right to get up in the pulpit and try to smooth over or amend anything that God has said about Himself. There is that passage about God hardening Pharaoh's heart. There have been books written to explain that away, but I will not explain it away. I will let it stand. If I don't understand it I will let it stand anyway. I believe what God says about Himself.

Then to worship correctly I must believe what God says about His Son. Not what some philosopher says about God's Son, or some theologian. I must believe what God says about His Son Jesus Christ our Lord. Then I must believe what God says about me. I must believe all the bad God says about me, and I also must believe all the good things He says He'll do for me. I must believe I'm as bad as God says I am and I must believe His grace is as great as He says it is.

Then I must believe whatever God says about sin. Here's another place where the psychologists and psychiatrists have done us great injury. They have euphonized sin. They call it a guilt complex. I believe that our trouble these days is that we've listened to the blandishments of these children of Adam and that we're afraid to see anybody get on his knees and get really scared.

Some of you have no doubt read of Peter Cartright, the great Methodist preacher who lived a century or so ago. Well, Peter was quite a preacher—an ignorant fellow, but God was on him. They tell how he once went to a conference and preached. The conference was in the charge of a little fellow from a seminary and of course Peter had little time for those boys. When Peter gave the invitation a lot of men came, including a big logger—a great big brawny fellow with monstrous, apelike arms, a huge fellow. He came down to the front and threw himself down and began to pray.

He'd been a sinner and he told God about it loudly, which scared this little seminary student half to death. He rant to him and said, "Compose yourself, brother, compose yourself." Peter Cartright pushed him aside, slapped the big logger on the back and said, "Pray on, brother, there's no composure in hell where you're going." Finally the man saw the goodness of God and the power of the cross, and the grace of God reached down and saved him. He leaped to his feet with a howl of delight and looked around for someone to hug and the first fellow he got hold of was the little seminary student. He picked him up and went dancing around at the top of his voice. It was hard on the young student's dignity, but perfectly right nevertheless.

Now it is possible to have religious experience without Jesus Christ. It's not only possible to have religious experience, it's possible to have worship without Jesus Christ. That is, it is possible for a man to have an experience of talking with God or being talked to by God. Look at Cain. Cain had a religious experience, but God did not accept him. Look at Balaam, son of Beor. He had an experience and yet God was not pleased with him. In an old Catholic church in Mexico I saw a pale-faced old lady come and kneel down before a statue of the Virgin. With her hands together and her eyes open and her face set in worship she was having a real religious experience, but it was in the presence of the Virgin Mary. In a church in the United States I saw a huge statue of the Virgin, much larger than any person here; her bare feet were extended so the worshipers could kiss them and her great toe on one foot had been worn down with the lips of those who came to worship.

Yes, it's possible to worship but not be accepted by God Almighty. Brethren, I'm not sure but that those old pagans who believed in the gods of Olympia and Valhalla, who called God Thor or Zeus, were having some kind of an experience; but they died and perished nevertheless. It is not an experience that saves us; it is the blood of the Lord Jesus Christ. Worship is not simply having a solemn feeling about the length of time and the brief duration of our lives on earth and the vastness of the heavens and the smallness of our bodies. That may be beautiful but it's not worship. To worship acceptably, I repeat, is to be born anew by the Holy Ghost through faith in the Lord Jesus Christ and have the Holy Spirit of Christ teach us to worship and enable us to worship.

> *We praise Thee, O God, we acknowledge Thee to be the Lord.*
> *All the earth doth worship Thee, the Father everlasting.*
> *To Thee all angels cry aloud, the heavens and all the powers*
>   *therein;*
> *To Thee Cherubim and Seraphim continually do cry,*
> *Holy, Holy, Holy, Lord God of Sabaoth:*
> *Heaven and earth are full of the majesty of Thy glory.*

The glorious company of the Apostles praise Thee.
The goodly fellowship of the Prophets praise Thee.
The noble army of Martyrs praise Thee.
The holy Church throughout all the world doth acknowledge
    Thee,
The Father of an infinite Majesty;
Thine adorable, true and only Son;
Also the Holy Ghost, the Comforter.

So says the old Te Deum.

Excerpt from
How to be Filled with the Holy Spirit

Who Is the Holy Spirit?

44

Who is the Holy Spirit?

We all use the word "spirit" a great deal. Now I want to tell you what I do and do not mean by it. In the first place, we rule out all of the secondary uses of the word "spirit." I do not mean courage, as when we say, "That's the spirit!" I don't mean temper or temperament or pluck. I mean nothing so nebulous as that. Spirit is a specific and identifiable substance. If not definable, it can at least be described. Spirit is as real as matter, but it is another mode of being than matter.

We are all materialists to some extent. We are born of material parents into a material world; we are wrapped in material clothes and fed on material milk and lie in a material bed, and sleep and walk and live and talk and grow up in a world of matter. Matter presses upon us obtrusively and takes over our thinking so completely that we cannot speak of spirit without using materialistic terms. God made man out of the dust of the ground, and man has been dust ever since, and we can't quite shake it off.

Matter is one mode of being; spirit is another mode of being as authentic as matter.

Material things have certain characteristics. For instance, they have weight. Everything that is material weighs something; it yields to gravitational pull. Then, matter has dimensions; you can measure the thing if it is made of matter. It has shape. It has an outline of some sort, no matter whether it is a molecule or an atom or whatever it may be, on up to the stars that shine. Then, it is extended in space. So I say that weight, dimension, shape and extension are the things that belong to matter. That is one mode of being; that is one way of existing.

One power of spirit, of any spirit (for I am talking about *spirit* now, not about the Holy Spirit), is its ability to penetrate. Matter bumps against other matter and stops; it cannot penetrate. Spirit can penetrate everything. For instance, your body is made of matter, and yet your spirit has penetrated your body completely. Spirit can penetrate spirit. It can penetrate personality—oh, if God's people could only learn that spirit can penetrate personality, that your personality is not an impenetrable substance, but can be penetrated. A mind can be penetrated by thought, and the air can be penetrated by light, and material things and mental things, and even spiritual things, can be penetrated by spirit.

Now, what is the Holy Spirit? Not *who*, but *what*? The answer is that the Holy Spirit is a Being dwelling in another mode of existence. He has not weight, nor measure, nor size, nor any color, no extension in space, but He nevertheless exists as surely as you exist.

The Holy Spirit is not enthusiasm. I have found enthusiasm that hummed with excitement, and the Holy Spirit was nowhere to be found there at all; and I have found the Holy Ghost when there has not been much of what we call enthusiasm present. Neither is the Holy Spirit another name for genius. We talk about the spirit of Beethoven and say, "This or that artist played with great spirit. He interpreted the spirit of the master." The Holy Spirit is none of these things. Now what is He?

He is a Person. Put that down in capital letters—that the Holy Spirit is not only a Being having another mode of existence, but He is Himself a Person, with all the qualities and powers of personality. He is not matter, but He *is* substance. The Holy Spirit is often thought of as a beneficent wind that blows across the Church. If you think of the Holy Spirit as being literally a wind, a breath, then you think of Him as nonpersonal and nonindividual. But the Holy Spirit has will and intelligence and feeling and knowledge and sympathy and ability to love and see and think and hear and speak and desire the same as any person has.

You may say, "I believe all that. You surely don't think you are telling us anything new!" I don't hope to tell you very much that is new; I only hope to set the table for you, arranging the dishes a little better and a little more attractively so that you will be tempted to partake. Many of us have grown up on the theology that accepts the Holy Spirit as a Person, and even as a divine Person, but for some reason it never did us any good. We are as empty as ever, we are as joyless as ever, we are as far from peace as ever, we are as weak as ever. What I want to do is to tell you the old things, but while I am doing it, to encourage your heart to make them yours now, and to walk into the living, throbbing, vibrating heart of them, so that from here on your life will be altogether different.

So the Spirit is a Person. That's *what* He is. Now, *who* is He?

The historic church has said that He is God. Let me quote from the Nicene Creed: "I believe in the Holy Ghost, the Lord and Giver of life, Which proceedeth from the Father and the Son, and with the Father and the Son together is worshipped and glorified."

That is what the Church believed about the Holy Ghost 1,600 years ago. Let's be daring for a moment. Let's try to think away this idea that the Holy Spirit is truly God. All right. Let's admit something else into the picture. Let's say, "I believe in one Holy Ghost, the Lord and Giver of life, who with the Father and the Son is to be worshiped and glorified." For the "Holy Ghost" let's put in "Abraham, the father of the faithful, who with the Father and the Son together is worshiped and glorified." That is a monstrous thing, and in your heart already there is a shocked feeling. You couldn't do it. You couldn't admit a mere man into the holy circle of the Trinity! The Father and the Son are to be worshiped and glorified, and if the Holy Spirit is to be included here He has to be equal to the Father and the Son.

Now let's look at the Athanasian Creed. Thirteen hundred years old it is. Notice what it says about the Holy Spirit: "Such as the Father is, such is the Son, and such is the Holy Ghost." Once more let's do that terrible thing. Let's introduce into this concept the name of a man. Let's put David in there. Let's say, "Such as the Father is, such also is the Son, and such is the hymnist David." That would be a shock like cold water in the face! You can't do that. And you can't put the archangel Michael in there. You can't say, "Such as the Father is, such also is the Son, and such is the archangel Michael." That would be a monstrous inconsistency, and you know it!

I have told you what the great creeds of the church say. If the Bible taught otherwise, I would throw the creeds away. Nobody can come down the years with flowing beard, and with the dust of centuries upon him, and get me to believe a doctrine unless he can give me chapter and verse. I quote the creeds, but I preach them only so far as they summarize the teaching of the Bible on a given subject. If there were divergency from the teachings of the Word of God I would not teach the creed; I would teach the Book, for the Book is the source of all authentic information. However, our fathers did a mighty good job of going into the Bible, finding out what it taught, and then formulating the creeds for us.

Now let's look at what our song writers and our hymnists believed. Recall the words the quartet sang this evening:

> *Holy Ghost, with light divine,*
> *Shine upon this heart of mine.*

Let's pray that prayer to Gabriel, to Saint Bernard, to D. L. Moody. Let's pray that prayer to any man or any creature that has ever served God. You can't pray that kind of prayer to a creature. To put those words into a hymn means that the one about whom you are speaking must be God.

> *Holy Ghost, with power divine,*
> *Cleanse this guilty heart of mine.*

Who can get into the intricate depths of a human soul, into the deep confines of a human spirit and cleanse it? Nobody but the God who made it! The hymn writer who said "Cleanse this guilty heart of mine" meant that the Holy Ghost to whom he prayed was God.

> *Holy Spirit, all divine,*
> *Dwell within this heart of mine;*
> *Cast down every idol throne,*
> *Reign supreme—and reign alone.*

The church has sung that now for about one hundred years. *"Reign supreme—and reign alone."* Could you pray that to anybody you know? The man who wrote that hymn believed that the Holy Ghost was God, otherwise he wouldn't have said, "Reign supreme, and reign all by Yourself." That is an invitation no man can make to anybody, except the Divine One, except God.

Now the Scriptures. Notice that I am trying to establish the truth that the Holy Spirit is not only a Person, but that He is a divine Person; not only a divine Person, but God.

In Psalm 139 the hymnist attributes omnipresence to the Holy Ghost. He says, "Whither shall I go from thy spirit? or whither shall I flee from thy presence?" and he develops throughout the 139th Psalm, a language that is as beautiful as a sunrise and as musical as the wind through the willows, the idea that the Spirit is everywhere, having the attributes of deity. He must be deity, for no creature could have the attributes of deity.

In Hebrews 9:14 there is attributed to the Holy Ghost that which is never attributed to an archangel, or a seraphim, or a cherubim, or an angel, or an apostle, or a martyr, or a prophet, or a patriarch, or anyone that has ever been created by the hand of God. It says, "Through the eternal Spirit," and every theologian knows that eternity is an attribute of no creature which deity has ever formed. The angels are not eternal; that is, they had a beginning, and all created things had beginning. As soon as the word "eternal" is used about a being it immediately establishes the fact that he never had a beginning, is not a creature at all, but God. Therefore, when the Holy Ghost says "the eternal Spirit" about Himself He is calling Himself God.

Again, the baptismal formula in Matthew 28 says, "Baptizing them in the name of the Father, and of the Son, and of the Holy Ghost." Now try to imagine putting the name of a man in there. "Baptizing them in the name of the Father and the Son and the Apostle Paul." You couldn't think it! It is horrible to contemplate! No man can be admitted into that closed circle of deity. We baptize in the name of the Father and the Son, because the Son is equal with the Father in His Godhead, and we baptize in the name of the Holy Ghost because the Holy Ghost is also equal with the Father and the Son.

You say, "You are just a Trinitarian and we are Trinitarians already." Yes, I know it, but once again I tell you that I am trying to throw emphasis upon this teaching.

How many blessed truths have gotten snowed under. People believe them, but they are just not being taught, that is all. I think of our experience this morning. Here was a man and his wife, a very fine intelligent couple from another city. They named the church to which they belonged, and I instantly said, "That is a fine church!" "Oh, yes," they said, "but they don't teach what we came over here for." They came over because they were ill and wanted to be scripturally anointed for healing. So I got together two missionaries, two preachers, and an elder, and we anointed them and prayed for them. If you were to go to that church where they attend and say to the preacher, "Do you believe that the Lord answers prayer and heals the sick?" he would reply, "Sure, I do!" He believes it, but he doesn't teach it, and what you don't believe strongly enough to teach doesn't do you any good.

It is the same with the fullness of the Holy Ghost. Evangelical Christianity believes it, but nobody experiences it. It lies under the snow, forgotten. I am praying that God may be able to melt away the ice from this blessed truth, and let it spring up again alive, that the Church and the people who hear may get some good out of it and not merely say "I believe" while it is buried under the snow of inactivity and nonattention.

Let us recapitulate. Who is the Spirit? The Spirit is God, existing in another mode of being than ourselves. He exists as a spirit and not as matter, for He is not matter, but He is God. He is a Person. It was so believed by the whole Church of Christ down through the years. It was so sung by the hymnists back in the days of the first hymn writers. It is so taught in the Book, all through the Old Testament and the New, and I have given you only a few proof texts. I could spend the evening reading Scriptures stating this same thing.

Now what follows from all this? Ah, there is an unseen Deity present, a knowing, feeling Personality, and He is indivisible from the Father and the Son, so that if you were to be suddenly transferred to heaven itself you wouldn't be any closer to God than you are now, for God is already here. Changing your geographical location would not bring you any nearer to God nor God any nearer to you, because the indivisible Trinity is present, and all that the Son is the Holy Ghost is, and all that the Father is the Holy Ghost is, and the Holy Ghost is in His Church.

What will we find Him to be like? He will be exactly like Jesus. You have read your New Testament, and you know what Jesus is like, and the Holy Spirit is exactly like Jesus, for Jesus was God and the Spirit is God, and the Father is exactly like the Son; and you can know what Jesus is like by knowing what the Father is like, and you can know what the Spirit is like by knowing what Jesus is like.

If Jesus were to come walking down this aisle there would be no stampede for the door. Nobody would scream and be frightened. We might begin to weep for sheer joy and delight that He had so honored us, but nobody would be afraid of Jesus; no mother with a little crying babe would ever have to be afraid of Jesus; no poor harlot being dragged by the hair of her head had to be afraid of Jesus—nobody! Nobody ever need to be afraid of Jesus, because He is the epitome of love, kindliness, geniality, warm attractiveness and sweetness. And that is exactly what the Holy Ghost is, for He is the Spirit of the Father and the Son. *Amen.*